Edited by Sally Smith **September–December 2018**

5 **'Prayer' by George Herbert**
Lisa Cherrett *3–16 September*

18 **The earth is the Lord's**
Fiona Stratta *17–30 September*

34 ***Hinds' Feet on High Places***
Sally Smith *1–14 October*

48 **Living lightly**
Sally Welch *15–28 October*

60 **Grateful**
Dorinda Miller *29 October–11 November*

74 **Winter food for thought**
Janet Lunt *12–25 November*

90 **The saints of Advent**
Anne Noble *26 November–9 December*

103 **Advent: anticipation and preparation**
Liz Hoare *10–23 December*

116 **See amid the winter's snow**
Andrea Skevington *24–30 December*

125 **As a Child: Hinder** Phil Steer

129 **Retreat in the city** Clare Black

The Bible Reading Fellowship
15 The Chambers, Vineyard
Abingdon OX14 3FE
brf.org.uk

The Bible Reading Fellowship (BRF) is a Registered Charity (233280)

ISBN 978 0 85746 610 5

Acknowledgements
Scripture quotations taken from The Holy Bible, New International Version (Anglicised edition) copyright © 1979, 1984, 2011 by Biblica. Used by permission of Hodder & Stoughton Publishers, a Hachette UK company. All rights reserved. 'NIV' is a registered trademark of Biblica. UK trademark number 1448790.

Scripture quotations taken from the Holy Bible, New Living Translation, copyright © 1996, 2004, 2007, 2013. Used by permission of Tyndale House Publishers, Inc., Carol Stream, Illinois 60188. All rights reserved.

Scripture quotations taken from the Holy Bible, English Standard Version, published by HarperCollins Publishers, © 2001 Crossway Bibles, a division of Good News Publishers. Used by permission. All rights reserved.

Scripture quotations from The New Revised Standard Version of the Bible, Anglicised edition, copyright © 1989, 1995 by the Division of Christian Education of the National Council of the Churches of Christ in the United States of America. Used by permission. All rights reserved.

The Living Bible copyright © 1971 by Tyndale House Foundation. Used by permission of Tyndale House Publishers Inc., Carol Stream, Illinois 60188. All rights reserved.

Extract from *As a Child* by Phil Steer, published by lulu.com, 2012.

Every effort has been made to trace and contact copyright owners for material used in this resource. We apologise for any inadvertent omissions or errors, and would ask those concerned to contact us so that full acknowledgement can be made in the future.

Printed by Gutenberg Press, Tarxien, Malta

Sally Smith writes...

Welcome to *Quiet Spaces*.

I wonder: what is your image of God? Our perceptions of who God is affect our relationship with God, our worship and our service. A view of a judgemental God will lead to an element of fear and anxiety to please and obey. An overemphasis on a loving God may lead to a reduction of awe and wonder at the mystery and might of God. I am always challenged at Christmas as I imagine holding the baby Jesus, fully human yet fully God, in my arms. How can I relate to a baby as the all-powerful and all-knowing God I worship?

Recently, I was also challenged to reconsider my reactions to God as female. I have previously thought that I didn't need to think of God as mother. I had a good relationship with my father and this enabled me to have a positive relationship with my heavenly Father – so why change that? Surely Mother God was for those who couldn't (for whatever valid reason) relate to a male God? Or maybe I was wrong! It was put to me that God is neither male nor female, so maybe I should be thinking of God as both male and female. Now there was a completely different approach. I had the opportunity to join in some worship that addressed God entirely as female and I discovered a whole new side of God.

It can be a useful exercise to consider who you think God is, and what your image of God is. But then to allow yourself to be challenged by that image. What isn't included in there? Consider some of the opposites to your usual ideas and then live with them for a week or so. You may find you deepen your relationship with the God you already know, but you may find you discover a previously hidden facet of a God we can never fully know and who holds great surprises for each of us.

As you work with this issue of *Quiet Spaces*, my prayer is that you may meet with God in new and surprising ways.

Writers in this issue

Lisa Cherrett is Production Editor at Bible Society, having worked as an editor at BRF for 19 years. She sings in a choir, writes haiku poetry when the inspiration strikes and enjoys making her own perfume. She blogs at **lisannie44.wordpress.com**.

Fiona Stratta is a Speech and Language therapist and Speech and Drama teacher. She has written *Walking with Gospel Women*, *Walking with Old Testament Women* and *Walking with Biblical Women of Courage* for BRF. In her writing, she desires to connect readers' spiritual journeys more closely with their daily lives.

Sally Smith enjoys creating spaces that enable encounters with God through leading Quiet Days and creating prayer corners and stations. She has led prayer groups in her local church, works as a spiritual director and writes and produces educational materials.

Sally Welch is Vicar of Charlbury with Shorthampton and Area Dean of Chipping Norton in the Diocese of Oxford. She is a writer and lecturer on spirituality, and is particularly interested in pilgrimage and labyrinth. She has made many pilgrimages both in England and Europe.

Dorinda Miller has been leading Quiet Days and retreats in the UK and overseas, across denominations, for many years. As well as running Staying in the Vine, a six-week course on prayer and spiritual disciplines, she is currently developing audio meditation resources for **www.into-deeper-waters.com**.

Janet Lunt creates and leads Quiet Days which often incorporate multisensory prayer stations. She is a musician, active in the musical aspect of worship, playing and composing, and runs St Peter's Hospice Community Choir in Bristol.

Anne Noble grew up on Merseyside and studied geology at Oxford and Toronto. She is an Associate Minister at Colton in the diocese of Lichfield and is married with two grown-up daughters. She still enjoys geology, reflecting on what we can hear and see of the God of all time through rocks. In her spare time, she loves gardening.

Liz Hoare is tutor in spiritual formation at Wycliffe Hall in Oxford. She teaches discipleship and prayer and has a special interest in spiritual direction. She is married to Toddy, a sculptor, and they have a son. Liz enjoys baking, the English countryside and looking after her chickens.

Andrea Skevington lives in Suffolk with her family. She writes for both adults and children, winning the Christian Book of the Year award (Speaking Volumes) for her retelling, *The Lion Classic Bible* (Lion Hudson, 2011). She also enjoys storytelling for children and running creative writing seminars for adults.

'Prayer' by George Herbert

Lisa Cherrett

'Prayer' by George Herbert

Prayer the Church's banquet, angels' age,
God's breath in man returning to his birth,
The soul in paraphrase, heart in pilgrimage,
The Christian plummet sounding heaven and earth;

Engine against the Almighty, sinner's tower,
Reversèd thunder, Christ-side-piercing spear,
The six-days world transposing in an hour,
A kind of tune, which all things hear and fear;

Softness, and peace, and joy, and love, and bliss,
Exalted manna, gladness of the best,
Heaven in ordinary, man well dressed,
The Milky Way, the bird of paradise,

Church-bells beyond the stars heard, the soul's blood,
The land of spices; something understood.

Introduction

Reflective

The poem called 'Prayer' by George Herbert (1593–1633), a poet and priest who lived and ministered in Bemerton near Salisbury, is composed entirely of short phrases that describe many different facets of prayer. It contains 27 images, so we will not be able to explore them all in detail here. Some of the images, I confess, I don't completely understand, and some resonate more with me than others do, so I shall focus closely on just a handful and leave the rest to one side (maybe for you to explore on your own).

My favourite or best-understood phrases will almost certainly be different from yours, but I hope we will find at least some common ground. Read through the poem a couple of times, and highlight the words that strike a chord with you – the phrases that best describe your own experiences of prayer and those that spark your imagination and encourage you to discover more.

The very first picture, 'Prayer the Church's banquet', perhaps does a good job of summing up the whole poem. It is a banquet of nourishing ideas about prayer. A banquet in Herbert's time would not have been a meal of several courses, following a prescribed formal pattern, one after the other. All types of food would have been presented on the table at once, buffet-style. If that makes you think of a church bring-and-share supper with soggy quiche and many cheesy Wotsits, think again! A banquet is a smorgasbord of tasty delights, from the familiar to the exotic – and that is exactly what George Herbert sets before us in this poem.

How many different types of prayer can you think of? A publication like *Quiet Spaces* is the perfect place to find a wide range of ways of praying. Presented with such a banquet, will you stick to familiar favourite foods, or will you take the chance to try a different flavour, perhaps a way of praying that belongs to a tradition you're not a part of? Here is the church's banquet laid out in front of you: don't go hungry!

'The Christian plummet, sounding heaven and earth'

Spotlight

This is a fascinating phrase, though it's hard to understand. To take a sounding means to measure the depth of a body of water. It would be done by throwing a rope into the sea, weighted at one end with lead (the 'plummet') and marked at intervals of two or more fathoms. But neither heaven nor earth is a body of water, and we generally think of heaven in terms of height rather than depth. Doesn't God say that he lives in 'a high and holy place' (Isaiah 57:15)?

Yet the psalmist writes, 'Deep calls to deep in the roar of your waterfalls' (Psalm 42:7), and the Lord's Prayer teaches us to say, 'Your will be done, on earth as it is in heaven' (Matthew 6:10). There's an equivalence here – a sense that heaven, where God dwells, and earth, which is our home, are matched in some way. The things we experience on earth are felt in the heart of God in heaven, and heaven's ways can be replicated on earth.

In prayer, we have the opportunity to dive deeper, with God, into the difficulties we face on earth. Dennis Lennon, in his book *Turning the Diamond: Exploring George Herbert's images of prayer* (SPCK, 2002), says that this is 'a "getting-to-the-bottom-of-things" plummet' and that 'the real business of prayer [is] penetration into the heart and essence of things' (p. 37). Have you ever prayed for God to reveal the root cause of a problem – to get the measure of it, to bring it to the surface? Then you have been using the prayer that 'sounds' earth, that gauges the depth. The good news is that there is a matching depth to be sounded in heaven. However deep the trouble or pain we are in, there are depths of grace and love in the heart of God to cover the pain and resolve the trouble.

'Sounding' prayer

Creative

Why not make a sounding rope to help you get the measure of a particular problem that is weighing on your mind? Perhaps you have a loved one in the grip of an addiction, or you are in a relationship with someone whom you find difficult to forgive.

Find a ball of string, some thick thread or a thin piece of rope and attach it to a large piece of paper or cardboard. Alternatively, you could just draw a measuring line. Then mark it off into sections. At the top, write down the aspects of the problem that are easily visible on the surface. Follow the line down, writing any underlying issues next to each section. Can you reach down to something that might be a root cause? The lowest depth might simply be a large question mark. If so, write next to it, 'God knows'.

As you pray about this situation, both today and in the coming months, build your faith in the fact that, however deep our sorrows, there is a depth of grace and healing in heaven to match them. Let 'deep call to deep' as you ask God to meet the needs you present to him, at the most fundamental level possible.

Keep your sounding rope for as long as you need it. You could journal on the paper or cardboard around it, jotting down answers to prayer and any new understandings that God shows to you as you continue to pray. Remember that 'neither height nor depth… will be able to separate us from the love of God that is in Christ Jesus our Lord' (Romans 8:39).

'Engine against the Almighty'

Reflective

There are some violent images of prayer in the fifth and sixth lines of Herbert's poem. The 'engine against the Almighty' is a picture of a siege engine, designed to propel heavy objects toward or over the fortified walls of a castle. It sounds unbiblical, even heretical. Is Almighty God a walled city, impregnable to anything except a violent assault? Where is the simplicity of Jesus' words, 'Ask and it will be given to you' (Luke 11:9)?

There may be a clue in the meaning of 'Ask' in this verse: it means 'Keep on asking'. Of course, God is the generous Father who longs to answer our prayers, but our actual experience is that prayer sometimes feels like battering down the walls of God's resistance. Maybe it shouldn't, but it does. There is more than one place in the Bible where we find people asking persistently and getting an answer. Think of Abraham bargaining with God for mercy on Sodom and Gomorrah, beating him down from 'fifty righteous people in the city' to 'only ten' (Genesis 18:23–32). Some years later, Jacob physically wrestled with God, finally insisting, 'I will not let you go unless you bless me' (Genesis 32:26). Then there is Jesus' parable of the widow and the judge, with the conclusion, 'And will not God bring about justice for his chosen ones, who cry out to him day and night?' (Luke 18:7).

If the 'engine against the Almighty' is persistent prayer, perhaps 'reversèd thunder' is loud, angry prayer. Thunder and lightning are traditionally imagined to be signs of God's anger at sin and the way it destroys human happiness and well-being. Sometimes, we too get angry about injustice or cruelty that we witness in the world, and we need to express that anger back to God. We can justifiably turn thunder back to God, asking him to act on behalf of those who are cruelly or unjustly treated.

When was the last time you dared to fire off a thunderous prayer? Have you ever turned a siege engine on to God in prayer? What happened? Write or draw your feelings about these images.

'Christ-side-piercing spear'

Reflective

This is yet another violent image of prayer, perhaps even more shocking and unpleasant than the two we've already considered. The spear thrust into Jesus' side on the cross was the last injury his body received, and, it might seem, an unnecessary one. We're told that blood and water flowed from the wound, proving that Jesus was really dead.

None of us would wish to imagine that we ourselves were the centurion who carried out this act. How can it be a picture of prayer? I think, to understand it, we need to focus on what that flow of blood and water represents – the forgiveness and healing poured out on us as the result of Jesus' self-giving death on the cross. Just as the spear thrust released this flow, perhaps our prayers in some way 'activate' God's mercy, compassion and forgiveness, bringing it raining down on our heads and the heads of the people we pray for.

Take a few minutes to meditate on these words from Isaiah 53:5:

> But he was pierced for our transgressions,
> he was crushed for our iniquities;
> the punishment that brought us peace was on him,
> and by his wounds we are healed.

If you feel guilty or sick inside, prayer may be for you the Christ-side-piercing spear that releases the gift of forgiveness and healing. Or perhaps you have a friend or family member who needs to know peace of mind and freedom from guilt. Your prayers of intercession could be the spear that releases God's grace for that person.

In prayer, bring yourself or your loved one to Jesus and pray for the flow of his forgiveness and peace into the places that need them.

'The six-days world, transposing in an hour'

Reflective

'The six-days world' is the whole of creation, from the light that God commanded at the very beginning to the teeming billions of living creatures, including ourselves. 'Transposing' is a musical term that means 'changing key'. If you're not musical, perhaps this image doesn't help you much: you could imagine it instead as changing colour or simply changing mood.

In an hour of prayer, then, as we intercede for the world or for just one aspect of it, we can find that our mood changes, or we see the world in a different light. To return to Herbert's musical metaphor, we feel that difficult circumstances seem more hopeful (a change from minor to major key), or our meditation reveals to us more clearly God's grief over his suffering world (a change from major to minor).

Can you, in prayer, gather up the whole world to God and, in faith, see it change in some way? Prayer changes the key, the colour, the mood, of the world's music.

Herbert's poem continues, in the next line, 'a kind of tune, which all things hear and fear'. Do we believe that our prayers are not only music to God's ears but also sing a melody to the whole creation, the 'six-days world'? Prayer tunes our spiritual ears to hear God, and, in ways we rarely imagine or experience, it tunes the ears of creation to know and honour God better.

Creation prayer

Creative

Which is your favourite 'day' of creation? Are you inspired to pray by any particular part of the created world? Perhaps sunrise, when darkness gives way once again to light, is a time when your thoughts turn naturally to God's provision of strength for a new day. Being alone, watching the sea-tide coming in or going out, can be a great way of meditating on the majesty of God. Or, if you're a city lover, walking through the crowded streets and looking at the faces of the people surrounding you might move you to compassion for all those who are made in the image of God but in whom that image has become unrecognisable.

Draw a circle on a large piece of paper or card and divide it into six segments. Write or draw in those segments something to represent the six 'days' of creation: light and darkness; sky; land, seas and plants; sun, moon and stars; sea creatures and birds; land creatures and human beings.

If you have a whole hour set aside for prayer, take ten minutes to focus on each part of the created world, praising God for it and asking him to 'transpose' it in some way – to bring new hope to it or change your attitude to it. Use your imagination, or perhaps think of something appropriate in the news today. For the sky, you might consider the effects of air pollution; for land creatures, you could pray for the work of animal rescue centres.

If you have only ten minutes to spare, choose one of the six segments to pray over. You could return to the others for ten minutes each on the following days.

As you conclude your prayer for each 'day', colour in the segment with changing shades of colour from pale to bright, or with different colours of the rainbow.

'Exalted manna'

Imaginative

By the time we get to 'exalted manna' in the third stanza, there has been a definite change of key in Herbert's thoughts. Manna was, of course, the food miraculously provided by God for the Israelites in the desert. It came to them noiselessly in the night, as they slept. They didn't need to work or fight for this provision. All they had to do was to walk out in the morning light and gather it from the ground. They didn't need to hoard it; indeed, they couldn't, because it went mouldy by the next day. Manna was easy pickings, straight from the hand of God.

Sometimes, prayer is an effortless kind of sustenance – just there for the taking, fresh every morning. 'Exalted' means 'lifted up', as the priest in some church traditions lifts up the bread at Holy Communion in blessing. Similarly, we lift up our easy, effortless prayers, and they are a blessing to ourselves and other people.

Today, close your eyes and imagine yourself walking around or across a field, empty except for a scattering of white crumbs of bread. As you picture yourself bending down and picking up each crumb, light and fragile, send a light and easy prayer of thanks or a simple request to God. Don't struggle; say the first thing that comes to mind. Each prayer need only be a few words.

Finish your prayer time by saying, 'Lord, accept these prayers in the name of Jesus, the bread of life.'

'The Milky Way'

Creative

After the exalted manna, George Herbert describes prayer as 'heaven in ordinary'. In prayer, heaven meets us in the everyday places. It seems, though, that Herbert uses these homely images as a springboard for much more exotic ideas. At a time with no artificial lights, the Milky Way would have been more clearly visible to Herbert than it is to us, with our electric light pollution – and it would have been much more majestic.

Abraham was gazing up at the countless stars when God said to him, 'So shall your offspring be' (Genesis 15:5). So, if prayer is the Milky Way, it's something to strike awe and wonder into the heart. It's the accumulation of many praises and petitions to God, answered by him with a promise of 'offspring' – the effects of our prayer that will live on when we are gone, just as the stars survive for so much longer than our mortal bodies do.

It is impossible for us to know the full effect of our prayers, whether we receive an obvious answer or whether we never know what might have happened. I often pray for TV personalities or strangers, with little hope of ever knowing how my prayers are answered. I'm sure many of us pray about situations of conflict worldwide – for 'everyone caught up in those terrible floods' or 'all the refugees' – and of course we rarely hear how God might have worked in those situations. We can only pray in faith, not knowing.

You could create your own Milky Way of prayer. Buy some sticky silver stars and dark-blue paper, or paint a long roll of paper in a dark colour. When you say a prayer whose outcome you may never know, stick a silver star on the dark background as a record of the 'offspring' God promises to us as we pray in faith.

'The bird of paradise'

Bible reading

Here is a picture of prayer that, for most of George Herbert's contemporaries, would have depended on pure imagination. We are privileged enough to be able to watch TV natural history programmes that bring fabulous creatures from faraway lands before our eyes in all their glorious colours. Herbert’s first readers would have heard explorers’ stories of the bird of paradise and would have invested it with a magical quality.

We can imagine a bird of paradise with long sweeping tail feathers and iridescent colours, changing with the light, rather as a prism of glass throws out different colours when its facets are turned toward the light. This cannot be an image of prayer as a shopping list or a simple ‘thank you’ for everyday gifts. It must be a picture of prayer as something that takes us into the glory of heaven. I have to admit that my prayer life is nothing like this!

The bird of paradise is sometimes, though, equated with the phoenix, the mythical bird of red and gold that is reborn from its own ashes. As such, it’s often seen as a symbol of resurrection. As an image of prayer, then, it might represent the rebirth of the soul from the ashes of our sometimes ruined lives. As we pray in times of distress, God may bring a shimmering new life from our suffering, spreading light in every direction.

Spend some time with the description of heaven in Revelation 4:1–8 or the new Jerusalem coming down to earth in Revelation 21:10—22:4. Leave your list of petitions to one side and let this scripture lead you into prayers of adoration, asking only that ‘your kingdom come on earth, as it is in heaven’. Be caught up in the majesty and glory of God.

‘Something understood’

Reflective/creative

This final image of prayer in Herbert’s poetic banquet makes me smile, because so many of his ideas are far from easy to understand. Prayer itself, in fact, can be hard to understand. Sometimes the very idea of it seems to make no sense at all, and many of our cries to God are about circumstances that are hard to reconcile with our faith in a good and loving Lord.

However, there are moments in prayer when we do feel that our hearts and minds are settled and peaceful and can simply rest in God's greater knowledge of our lives. This experience can be like a shaft of sunlight breaking through the clouds. Perhaps Paul felt like this when he asked God three times to remove the thorn in his flesh that troubled him, and was told, 'My grace is sufficient for you, for my power is made perfect in weakness' (2 Corinthians 12:7–9).

Or perhaps there is another meaning to this phrase – that as we pray, there is 'something understood' by God. Paul writes, 'We do not know what we ought to pray for, but the Spirit himself intercedes for us through wordless groans. And he who searches our hearts knows the mind of the Spirit' (Romans 8:26–27).

Do you feel you've come to an understanding of some aspect of prayer that you didn't have before reading this poem by George Herbert? Can you pick out one or two favourite images from the 27 in the poem – either images that we've looked at in these notes or from among those we have not touched upon?

Try writing your own insights on prayer in the form of a poem, or choose the one of Herbert's images that intrigues you most and journal your thoughts about it.

Conclusion

Liturgy

George Herbert covers so many aspects of prayer, calling on so many different senses and abstract ideas, that his poem may seem overwhelming in its complexity. With 'something understood', it comes to rest after a long journey.

You could pray through your travels with the poem using the following words:

In the flavours of the church's banquet,
both familiar and untried,
Lord, hear our prayer.

In the matching depths of heaven and earth,
where we ask for your will to be done,
Lord, hear our prayer.

In the sound and fury of siege and thunder,
when we cry out to you night and day,
Lord, hear our prayer.

In the piercing pain of guilt and fear,
when we need your forgiveness and mercy poured out upon us,
Lord, hear our prayer.

As we hold our fragmented world before you,
asking for transformation,
Lord, hear our prayer.

In our ordinary requests for daily bread,
our petitions whose answers we may never see,
and our expressions of adoration and wonder,
Lord, hear our prayer.

May we come to an understanding of your ways,
just as ours are fully understood by you.
In Jesus' name. Amen

The earth is the Lord's

Fiona Stratta

The earth is the Lord's

Introduction

> Celebrate this festival to honour the Lord your God… for it is he who blesses you with bountiful harvests and gives you success in all your work. This festival will be a time of great joy for all.
>
> DEUTERONOMY 16:15

Harvest is a time of praise and worship as we celebrate the fruitfulness and beauty of the earth. It can also be a time to search out the wisdom inherent in creation, as Job recommended, 'Speak to the earth, and it will instruct you' (Job 12:8).

Although we often think of harvest in relation to crops, the harvest of the world's resources is far broader than this: 'The earth is the Lord's and the fullness thereof, the world and those who dwell therein' (Psalm 24:1, ESV). We are going to explore this 'fullness': the harvest above and below the earth's surface, the fields, the trees, the birds, the fish, the insects, the animals, for 'the glory of the Lord fills the whole earth' (Numbers 14:21, NIV).

'All things come from you, and of your own have we given you' (1 Chronicles 29:14, ESV). Awareness of this challenges us to live gratefully, humbly and with awe. It also calls us to live responsibly as stewards of all God gives us. Drawing aside for quiet, in a reflective and prayerful space with God, renews and recharges us. This then enables us to engage more fully, justly and mercifully in the world through his love and strength. Whatever affects the earth affects those who live in it, especially the poor. We can't do everything – that feels overwhelming – but we can do something. I have found that, even in small ways, this participation with God in caring for creation brings joy and satisfaction. As we go through this series, there are suggestions as to how we can move beyond our reflections on harvest by responding with action.

As we meditate, we are transformed. Write out any or all of the above verses and place them in a prominent position so that you can return to these words over the coming days.

Harvest of the fields: food

Creative

> Celebrate the Festival of Harvest when you bring me the first crops of your harvest... Celebrate the Festival of the Final Harvest at the end of the harvest season.
>
> EXODUS 23:16

Fifty days of barley harvest, starting at Passover, preceded the start of the wheat harvest. The Israelites travelled to Jerusalem in order to offer two loaves of bread baked with the first of their harvest's wheat flour. Alongside barley and wheat, other first fruits were brought – figs, grapes, pomegranates, olives and dates. The joyful procession to the temple was accompanied by the singing of psalms. The Feast of Tabernacles, the Final Harvest when all the crops were gathered in, was also a pilgrimage festival of rejoicing.

These are the backdrop to our Christian Harvest celebrations. Lammas Day (loaf mass) is still celebrated in some country areas on 1 August. Traditionally, it was a day when small loaves were taken to the church for a mass or communion service and offered in thanksgiving at the beginning of the harvest. Why not prayerfully bake some bread (or buy some) and share it with friends in a simple meal and reflection?

Say the words,

Be gentle when you touch bread.
Let it not lie uncared for, unwanted;
So often bread is taken for granted.
There is such beauty in bread.
Beauty of sun and soil,
Beauty of patient toil.
Wind and rain have caressed it,
Christ often blessed it –
Be gentle when you touch bread.

Source unknown; first printed in the *Australian Church Standard* and then reprinted in *The Living Church*, Volume 102, 1942

Look at the processional psalms (120—134) and choose one to praise God.

Finish with the words, 'You allow them to produce food from the earth – wine to make them glad, olive oil to soothe their skin, and bread to give them strength' (Psalm 104:14–15).

Organisations such as Tearfund are campaigning to reduce food wastage by encouraging individuals to refrain from buying surplus food which is then discarded, and by urging supermarkets to change policies that currently encourage shoppers to overbuy. You may like to look at their websites and sign up for one of their campaigns.

Harvest of the fields: clothes

Reflective

Start by slowly reading Matthew 6:28–33. Thank God for his provision for you.

In the Bible, we read of wool and flax being harvested, spun and woven for clothes of wool and linen.

What is the oldest item in your wardrobe? Why has it stood the test of time? What is your favourite item? Why?

In the UK, we consume 400% more clothes than two decades ago. Around 85% of clothes are made by women and 97% are made abroad. Cheap labour frequently violates workers', women's and human rights. Women in the clothes production industry are often caught in a poverty trap. Although globalisation has meant cheaper clothes for consumers, this has been not only at a human cost, but also at an environmental cost. For example, much cotton is genetically modified using vast amounts of chemicals.

Now think again about the item of clothing you chose. Imagine the different processes and people that were involved in its creation. Thank God for them and their labour on your behalf.

How do we live righteously when it comes to clothing today? We can show that we value people and the planet by our everyday decisions: looking out for and buying locally made clothing, fair trade clothing and organic clothing; letting the brands and shops we buy from know that we care about the workers producing our clothes; refusing to be wasteful with our textiles. We are not powerless but those making our clothes often are.

You may like to go to **www.truecostmovie.com** from where the above statistics were taken.

Harvest of the trees

Going out

> Then God said, 'Look! I have given you every seed-bearing plant throughout the earth and all the fruit trees for your food.'
>
> GENESIS 1:29

Many trees are mentioned in the Bible, useful for their wood (such as the cedars of Lebanon) and their fruits, such as the pomegranate, fig, palm and olive. The olive tree is a wonderful tree and was important in biblical times: its wood was used to make small and large objects; its fruit was eaten; its oil was used for eating, cooking, anointing, in worship, and as a healing balm; its leaves have medicinal properties. The palm tree also gives much: fruit; wine from the sap; leaf stems used to make ropes and rigging; leaves used for many different articles and to provide shade; tall, straight trunks valuable for their timber. It is known as the tree of life to desert people.

Take a walk in some woodland if you are able, enjoying the variety of trees. Use some wax crayons to do some bark rubbing, noticing the patterns and textures as you work. Trees have stability – they remind us that we need to stay rooted in Christ where we can flourish. As you walk, meditate on the following verses:

> But I am like an olive tree, thriving in the house of God. I will always trust in God's unfailing love.
>
> PSALM 52:8

> But the godly will flourish like palm trees and grow strong like the cedars of Lebanon.
>
> PSALM 92:12

> Even in old age they will still produce fruit; they will remain vital and green.
>
> PSALM 92:14

If you are unable to go out, enjoy the feel and look of wooden objects in your home. Trace the grain in the wood with your finger as you dwell on the above verses.

We hear much spoken about the need to preserve the trees of the world's rainforests. There are also projects much closer to home. Look at the Woodland Trust's website (**www.woodlandtrust.org.uk**). A positive step is to reduce one's carbon footprint as much as possible (for example, by reducing food waste, increasing recycling, buying goods in environmentally friendly packaging, buying seasonal and local food, supporting clean energy) and then to offset the remaining carbon footprint by planting trees that will take carbon dioxide out of the atmosphere. To find out more, visit **www.climatestewards.org**, **www.footprint.wwf.org.uk** or **www.wordforest.org**.

Harvest for essential oils, ointments, medicines and spices

Reflective

> On each side of the river grew a tree of life, bearing twelve crops of fruit, with a fresh crop each month. The leaves were used for medicine to heal the nations.
>
> REVELATION 22:2

Many essential oils, ointments, medicines and spices can be harvested from plants and trees. God gives us harvests for our sustenance and also for our enjoyment and well-being. Certain fragrances evoke memories that bring us much pleasure; scents can relax and arouse. Many are mentioned in the Bible: myrrh, frankincense, aloes, cinnamon, saffron, calamus, henna, cassia, cinnamon, aloes and balm. Some had specific uses, such as myrrh for burial and for beautification, and frankincense to symbolise God's presence.

If you have an oil burner, burn your favourite oil. If not, you could light a fragranced candle. Reflect on the words from the hymn 'Lord of all Hopefulness' by Jan Struther (1931): 'Lord of all gentleness, Lord of all calm, whose voice is contentment, whose presence is balm'. Balm was a healing resin from a tree. Enjoy the Lord's soothing and healing presence.

Harvest below the earth

Creative

> The silver is mine, and the gold is mine, says the Lord of Heaven's Armies.
>
> HAGGAI 2:8

In the making of jewellery, God's treasures and human creativity are combined. In Exodus 35, we read that Bezalel was filled with the Spirit and given the wisdom and ability to work in many crafts, including metals and precious stones.

Below the earth is much to harvest that is of great beauty. Silver, gold, iron, copper, lapis lazuli, onyx, crystal, coral, jasper, rubies, peridot and precious stones are all mentioned in Job 28. Some have practical value, such as for ironwork and copper utensils, and others are of decorative value. Used to adorn the tabernacle and temple, their beauty pointed to a God who is infinitely more beautiful. Of much greater value than precious metals and gemstones is the wisdom that leads us to thirst for God himself. You may like to read Job 28.

Take an item of jewellery or ornament containing a gemstone. Such items often symbolise the love that others have for us. Enjoy its beauty and then thank God for his wisdom, of even greater value, promised to those who ask for it.

Is there an art or craft that you enjoy? Spend some time carrying out this activity, praising God as you do so for the God-given ability to learn and practise this skill and for the joy it gives you.

The beauty and bounty of the precious stones and metals within the earth should be for all, not just the consumer. Yet some mines are full of adults and children being exploited in terrible conditions. There are mine-owners who pay no attention to the environmental impact of their industry and jewellers who ignore the plight of those sourcing their gems. However, there are people creating ethical, fair-trade jewellery where the human rights of those mining have been considered and the environment protected. Next time you buy a piece of jewellery, consider asking whether the product can be traced back to its source. You may like to look at **www.gregvalerio.com**.

Harvest of the waters

Imaginative

> You gave them charge of everything you made, putting all things under their authority... the fish in the sea, and everything that swims the ocean currents.
>
> PSALM 8:6, 8

We read of fish in several of the gospel narratives, miracles and parables. Step now into Peter's shoes (based on John 21:1–7):

It had been my idea, the night's fishing. But I couldn't even seem to fish any more. As we were returning with empty nets, we saw a figure on the shore. He instructed us to throw the net to the right of the boat. It was hard to believe that he could see a shoal of fish from so far away in the dim rays of dawn, but we had nothing to lose, so we followed his advice.

Then it happened – the nets filled with fish, so many that we couldn't pull them into the boat. We would have to drag them to shore. Deep within my memory, something stirred – I recalled the master sitting in my boat watching Andrew and me pulling in such a vast quantity of fish that our nets were breaking, saw myself fall at the Lord's feet in shame, heard him say that I would fish for men.

At that same moment, John turned to me and said, 'It is the Lord.' I put on my tunic, dived in and swam for shore – no walking on water this time – nothing to prove, every iota of pride now gone, just wanting to be in his presence, hear his voice, let him know that I loved him, a longing to be restored.

Enjoy looking at photographs of the sea, or alternatively watch a film clip – there are so many awe-inspiring ones to choose from on YouTube. If you live close enough, go on a prayer walk beside the sea. Allow yourself to be restored by the beauty of the sounds and sights, enjoying the presence of the Lord, as Peter did. Praise God for our oceans and all that we harvest from them. Then pray that we will not overuse or under-protect our seas and that they will be managed equitably and sustainably.

Caring for the rivers, lakes and oceans and fishing them wisely is essential for their and our long-term future. We can join others in speaking out against chemical pollution, over-fishing, wasteful fishing and the dumping of plastic that damages the oceans and their creatures. You may like to look at **www.plasticoceans.org**. Consider purchasing only certified, sustainable seafood. Look for the MSC (Marine Stewardship Council) logo; such fish have been caught with minimal environmental damage and from responsibly managed sources.

Harvest of the insects

Creative

> I would satisfy you with wild honey from the rock.
>
> PSALM 81:16

Various insects are harvested in different parts of the world and are important for their nutritional value. They are also an essential part of the food chain. In addition to this, insects decompose organic matter, pollinate crops and flowers, and help to control pests.

The bee is of fundamental importance to our well-being as human beings. In Britain, bees pollinate 75 per cent of our food and crops. Because of them, our harvest flourishes. As well as being a natural sweetener, honey has anti-inflammatory, anti-bacterial and anti-septic qualities. It contains minerals and vitamins and is said to improve the quality of sleep, hair, skin and nails.

Try using honey as your only sweetener for a few days in order to appreciate this incredible resource. Each time you use it, thank God for the bee and all that it gives us. Watch one of the many fascinating YouTube clips about the working life of bees and the making of honey.

Bake a honey cake to share with friends. While cooking, ponder on the following verses:

> How sweet your words taste to me; they are sweeter than honey.
>
> PSALM 119:103

> My child, eat honey, for it is good, and the honeycomb is sweet to the taste. In the same way, wisdom is sweet to your soul. If you find it, you will have a bright future, and your hopes will not be cut short.
>
> PROVERBS 24:13–14

Habitat loss, intensive farming, the use of harmful pesticides, climate change and invasive species have all played a part in reducing the bee population. As a result, 35 species of bee are under threat of extinction. Some profit-making honey harvesters take off too much honey from the hives, leaving insufficient to see the colony through the next winter. However, we can have a positive impact on this wonderful part of God's creation by buying honey locally from sources where there is balanced beekeeping, with an emphasis on the well-being and natural behaviour of the bees; looking out for fair-trade honey; or growing spring and summer flowers that are bee friendly. You may be interested in obtaining a Bee Saver Kit that both educates and enables us to create the right environment to encourage bees. Visit **www.foe.co.uk/bees**.

Harvest from animals

Creative

> The godly care for their animals, but the wicked are always cruel.
>
> PROVERBS 12:10

The first recorded animal conservation project was carried out by Noah (Genesis 6—9). In this account, we learn that every living creature is important to God. God told Noah that he had given him animals and fish for food, along with vegetables and grain, reminding Noah that all creatures were in his care.

St Francis of Assisi (1181–1226), founder of the Franciscan friars, cared passionately for all God's creatures. He looked on them as objects of love reflecting their maker. St Francis lived as simply as he could, caring for and preaching to the poor.

One of St Francis's most famous sayings is 'Start by doing what's necessary; then do what's possible; and suddenly you are doing the impossible.' Do an online image search for 'Start by doing what is necessary'. You will find that there are many images with this quote. Enjoy looking at them. How do they encourage you? How do they challenge you? Which is your favourite? Why? Remembering this quote can encourage us as we seek to live in ways that involve caring for all of God's creation. Write out the quote in your journal in a decorative or colourful way and prayerfully see how this speaks to you.

You may like to consider the source of the meat you eat. How have the cows, pigs, sheep and goats that give us meat and dairy products been reared and cared for? We can use both our voice and our purchasing power. Charities such as Tearfund (**www.tearfund.org**) provide schemes by which we can help to improve the diet and living standards of people in poor countries by giving them animals to rear and breed.

Harvest of the birds

Imaginative/going out

> The birds... sing among the branches of the trees.
>
> PSALM 104:12

Different people groups have certain birds and eggs in their diets. Throughout history, various birds have been eaten and some overeaten to extinction. Birds are of crucial importance for their dispersal of seeds.

The Bible mentions birds on many occasions. Perhaps the most dramatic narrative involving birds is when God fed the Israelites with quail. Enter into this event imaginatively (based on Exodus 16:1–13):

We had been free of the Egyptians for a whole month. Perhaps that should have been a cause for celebration, but we were so hungry. We could not eat all of our animals, for we would have none left for breeding to maintain our flocks. Although afflicted in Egypt, we had always had enough food there: fruit, vegetables, slowly stewed meat and a constant supply of bread. Now we were facing starvation. What had been the point of it all? Was the Lord really in all this?

So we began to grumble to each other, and then finally to Moses and Aaron. So desperate were we at the thought of dying out in the desert, that we actually wished we had been killed by the Lord back in Egypt.

But the Lord was gracious to us in our despair; he instructed Moses and Aaron and they told us that we would eat meat that very evening and then all the bread we wanted the next morning. More than that, we were to see the awesome glory of the Lord in the cloud. It was breathtakingly beautiful, silencing every murmur of complaint and fear. That evening we saw in the distance another cloud, or so it seemed. As it neared, we perceived that this moving cloud was a flock of quail… thousands upon thousands of them. They seemed to fall out of the sky! Child and adult joyfully ran to pick them up and we were fed.

Contemplate a time in your life when God has provided for you in a special way. The assurance of God's presence in times of great need is often as important as the provision. God who notices the falling of a sparrow surely cares for us.

Take a walk where you can listen to birdsong; if you are unable to do this, listen to birdsong on YouTube. Let their beautiful songs lead you to worship God.

Have the chickens producing our eggs been kept in natural conditions or in overcrowded sheds with no sunlight? How have the chickens we eat been reared? We can look out for four labels as consumers: free range; organic; RSPCA freedom food;

higher welfare. Take a look at the 'Chicken out' project at **www.rivercottage.net/campaigns/chicken-out**.

Harvest in our lives

Poetry

This excerpt from a well-known hymn reminds us that all the wonders of the created world tell of God's glory and lead us to praise him. Singing is the harvest from our mouths – the 'fruit of our lips' (Hosea 14:2, NIV).

> *All things bright and beautiful,*
> *All creatures great and small,*
> *All things wise and wonderful,*
> *The Lord God made them all.*
>
> *He gave us eyes to see them,*
> *And lips that we might tell*
> *How great is God Almighty,*
> *Who has made all things well.*
>
> Cecil Frances Alexander (1848)

Harvest is frequently used as a metaphor in the Bible regarding our lives, such as reaping what we sow, producing the fruit of righteousness and the fruit of the Spirit. The following excerpt from 'Come, ye thankful people, come' reminds us that God is Lord of both the physical and spiritual harvest.

> *Lord of Harvest, grant that we*
> *Wholesome grain and pure may be.*
> *Even so, Lord, quickly come,*
> *Bring thy final harvest home;*

Gather thou thy people in
Free from sorrow, free from sin.
Henry Alford (1844)

Praise God through song, offering the fruit of your lips. Pray that you will be wholesome grain.

Resting in 'the God of nature'

Poetry

'The Pulley' by George Herbert (1633)

When God at first made man,
Having a glass of blessings standing by,
'Let us,' said he, 'pour on him all we can.
Let the world's riches, which dispersèd lie,
Contract into a span.'

So strength first made a way;
Then beauty flowed, then wisdom, honour, pleasure.
When almost all was out, God made a stay,
Perceiving that, alone of all his treasure,
Rest in the bottom lay.

'For if I should,' said he,
'Bestow this jewel also on my creature,
He would adore my gifts instead of me,
And rest in Nature, not the God of Nature;
So both should losers be.

'Yet let him keep the rest,
But keep them with repining restlessness;
Let him be rich and weary, that at least,
If goodness lead him not, yet weariness
May toss him to my breast.'

Restlessness is part of the human condition, as Solomon recognised. In spite of the joy and wonder at all we can harvest and enjoy, this poem reveals that God will not allow us to be fully content with what he has given us materially. I saw a pulley at work recently in an old mill; as the rope was pulled down, the heavy bag of barley was lifted to the top of the mill, ready to be poured into the grinding machine. By pulling one force down, another was lifted. The restlessness that pulls us down is stilled by the spiritual rest that only God can give, which lifts us as it quietens us.

Hinds' Feet on High Places

Sally Smith

The story

Introduction

Hinds' Feet on High Places (quotations from Kingsway, 1982, reprinted 2003) is an allegorical story written in the 1950s by Hannah Hurnard. As the opening sentence says,

> This is the story of how Much-Afraid escaped from her Fearing relatives and went with the Shepherd to the High Places where 'perfect love casteth out fear'.

She lives in the village of Much-Trembling in the Valley of Humiliation, which is as unpleasant a place to live as it sounds.

At the start of the story, the main character, Much-Afraid, is already in the service of the Chief Shepherd, but we read of her journey to overcome the many trials and barriers she meets as she tries to reach the High Places where she will be made whole (she walks with a limp and is, as her name suggests, much-afraid). The Shepherd tells her:

> The High Places... are the *starting point* for the journey down to the lowest place in the world. When you have hind's feet and can go 'leaping on the mountains and skipping on the hills', you will be able, as I am, to run down from the heights in gladdest self-giving and then go up to the mountains again.

> You will be able to mount to the Highest Places swifter than eagles, for it is only up on the Highest Places of Love that anyone can receive the power to pour themselves down in an utter abandonment of self-giving.
>
> p. 37

So Much-Afraid journeys to the High Places and is healed in every sense and is then able to return to the valley to serve the Shepherd in new ways.

At times, the imagery can seem clumsy and forced, but if you allow the images to speak in their own language, they can give a helpful way of seeing our journey with and towards God. I have kept the names used in the book and suggest you let them mean what they do for you, and accept that this may change. It may be that they have a meaning you are not able to put into words, but which is significant for you. I have avoided interpreting where the High Places are, giving you the freedom to translate it into your words, or keep it as a concept outside words, and maybe outside understanding.

Reread the quote above from page 37. As you read, notice your response. Do you long to run and leap on the Highest Places of Love? Allow God to transport you to those places and spend time there with the Chief Shepherd.

Much-Afraid

Creative

All the characters in the book are named to reflect their character, so the main character is Much-Afraid, but we also meet Craven Fear, Resentment, Self-Pity, Sorrow and Suffering and Gloomy. It is towards the end of the book when Much-Afraid reaches the peaks of the High Places that we meet some more positive characters in

Joy, Peace, Grace and Glory and Praise and Thanksgiving. When she reaches the High Places, Much-Afraid becomes Grace and Glory, but I think she has many other positive characteristics, and so also other names, even when she is living in the Valley of Humiliation. She is Loyal to the Shepherd and to her neighbours, she is Longing to go to the High Places and she Sings the songs in the Shepherd's book.

What one name would describe you? Would other people suggest a different name to the one you would prefer? What other names might you also be known by?

On a piece of paper, maybe using different coloured pens, write some of the 'names' you might be known by and that you see yourself as. They may be a mixture of what we might describe as positive and negative, but that's okay.

Spend some time with those names, noticing how you feel about each one, which you would like to get rid of and which you would like to be more widely known. Offer the names to God, the Chief Shepherd, who calls each of us by name and has our names engraved on the palm of his hand. Listen to the names he uses for you.

Talk to God about any names that are not on your paper that you wish were.

Much-Afraid says:

> 'He will never be content until He makes me what He is determined that I ought to be,' and because she was still Much-Afraid and not yet ready to change her name, she added with a pang of fear, 'I wonder what He plans to do next, and if it will hurt very much indeed?'
>
> p. 112

Shortcomings

Reflective

> In the first place she was a cripple, with feet so crooked that they often caused her to limp and stumble as she went about her work. She had also the very unsightly blemish of a crooked mouth which greatly disfigured both expression and speech and was sadly conscious that these blemishes must be a cause of astonishment and offence to many who knew that she was in the service of the great Shepherd. Most earnestly she longed to be completely delivered from these shortcomings and to be made beautiful, gracious, and strong as were so many of the shepherd's other workers, and above all to be made like the Chief Shepherd Himself.
>
> p. 11

Remember this is an allegory, so the disfigurements and disabilities of Much-Afraid are symbols of some of the things that stop her from functioning as well as she might. She is expressing a longing to be able to serve the Shepherd better if only she were different. How often do we long to be different, to be more like that person, or to be able to deal with situations in the easy way this person does?

It takes Much-Afraid huge courage to set out and be prepared to be changed on her journey. It then takes perseverance to continue the journey and not be tempted to return to her little cottage.

What are the things that stop you doing all that you could do in service of the Shepherd? What stops you being the person he would have you be? As you sit with God, tell him of the things that get in the way and be courageous enough to offer some of them to him, asking that he removes them.

One of the things Much-Afraid tells the Shepherd she has learnt along the way is this:

> You, my Lord, never regarded me as I actually was, lame and weak and crooked and cowardly. You saw me as I would be when You had done what You promised and had brought me to the High Places... You always treated me with the same love and graciousness as though I were a queen already and not wretched little Much-Afraid... My Lord, I cannot tell You how greatly I want to regard others in the same way.
>
> p. 149

The Fearings family

Reflective

Much-Afraid is a member of the Fearings family. They are concerned about her serving the Shepherd, and when she starts on the journey they send family members after her to get her to come back and marry Craven Fear. As she journeys further, they become more calculated in their approach and send appropriate members of the family to talk to her, each using their own strengths such as Self-Pity, Resentment, Bitterness and Pride. The Shepherd tells her not to let them 'begin painting a picture on the screen of your imagination' or she will 'walk with fear and trembling and agony, where no fear is' (p. 91).

So, one of the big lessons Much-Afraid learns on her journey is not to let her Fearing relatives in. The Shepherd tells her she should not have let them into her cottage and, as they appear on her journey, she learns to ignore them, say no to them, and call for the Shepherd when they appear. Some people find it helpful to see the distractions and temptations they face as people and to deal with them as they would an annoying phone call – firmly but politely to say 'Go away', and to call for reinforcements if it all gets too much.

As you go through the next day, watch out for times when you are tempted to be distracted from the service of the Shepherd. Send the distractions away and call on the Shepherd to be with you.

The seed of true love

Creative

Before anyone can enter the Kingdom of Love in the High Places, they need to have the flower of Love blooming in their hearts. Much-Afraid is honest when she looks in her heart, then says to the Shepherd, 'I don't think I see the kind of Love that you are talking about, at least, nothing like the love which I see in you' (p. 16). So, at the start of the journey, he plants the seed of true Love in her heart, giving it time to grow and develop before she reaches the High Places. The seed is in the form of a thorn which he holds in his scarred hands, with the thorn being the exact shape and size of the scar in his palms.

> To love does mean to put your SELF into the power of the loved one and to become very vulnerable to pain.
>
> p. 16

Take some threads or wools and plait them together into a wristband. As you work, talk to Jesus about the pain of love and the joy of love and ask for his seed of love to grow in you. You may want to add a bead or special knot to represent the seed of love. Wear your wristband as a reminder of that seed planted in you.

Transfiguration

Imaginative

Towards the end of the journey, the Shepherd takes Much-Afraid up a mountain where, with strong echoes of the Transfiguration in Matthew 17, he is transfigured and she recognises him for who she had believed him to be all along. The following is a mixture of the two transfigurations.

Imagine climbing a mountain with Jesus. He may be carrying you, or you may walk easily together in single file or side by side. Look around you, listen and smell the freshness of the air. See the white peaks in the distance.

When you get to the top, pause and admire the view.

Then you see him become who you have always sensed him to be, 'the King of Love Himself, King of the whole realm of Love. He [is] clothed in a white garment glistening in its purity, but over it He [wears] a robe of purple and blue and scarlet studded with gold and precious stones. On his head he [wears] the crown royal' (p. 118).

You bow down at his feet to worship.

When you are ready, look up into his face. There you see that the face looking down at you is the same face of Jesus who walked with you, or carried you up the mountain.

Then, together, you look out over the Kingdom of Love. What can you see? Can you see your home and places you recognise? Wherever the King of Love has travelled, you see beautiful white flowers blossom. Notice and enjoy seeing his love at work across the world.

When you are ready, come down from the mountain. You may wish to write about your experience in your journal.

The Shepherd's book of songs

Reflective

Throughout the book, Much-Afraid recalls and sings songs she has learnt from the book the shepherds used. Often, as she sings, she discovers that the words take on a new meaning or seem more appropriate and real than they have done before. After the seed of Love has been planted in her heart:

> Songs of joy were welling up in her innermost being. And the songs which best expressed this new happiness and thankfulness were from the old book which the shepherds so loved to use as they worked among the flocks and led them to the pastures.
>
> p. 23

Are there songs that you return to regularly? They may reflect your mood or they may have the capacity to move you to a fresh and more joyful place when life feels tough.

Start singing one of those songs now, and return to it during the day, noticing the effect it has on you and allowing it to draw you closer to God.

Hinds' feet

Meditative

The title for the book is taken from two Bible passages.

> He maketh my feet like hinds' feet, and setteth me upon my high places.
>
> PSALM 18:33, KJV

Or, as *The Message* puts it: 'Now I run like a deer; I'm king of the mountain.'

And from Habakkuk 3:19:

> God, the Lord, is my strength;
> he makes my feet like the feet of a deer,
> and makes me tread upon the heights.

If you watch deer running, they do so effortlessly, over any terrain and up hills and mountains. You can look on YouTube for some examples.

Much-Afraid watches the Shepherd running off:

> He leapt on to a great rock at the side of the path and from there to another and yet another, swifter than almost her eyes could follow His movements. He was leaping up the mountains, springing from height to height, going on before them until in a moment or two He was lost to sight.
>
> p. 43

She knows that at first she is not able to keep up with him, but believes that later she will be able to leap across the mountains with him.

Read Psalm 18:31–50.

Now read it again, but slowly, and allow a word or phrase to catch your attention. When it does, stop and stay with it, repeating it slowly and allowing it to enter you and become part of you.

When you are ready, leave it and move on until the next word or phrase catches you.

You might want to record the words you've spent time with in your journal.

Who is God?

Creative

In Psalm 18, which gives the book its title, we read 'For who is God except the Lord?' (v. 31). Here, the psalmist explores who God is for him, using the imagery of the rock, fortress, deliverer, shield, horn of salvation and stronghold. He then goes on to describe what God has done for his people and then for the individual writer, which naturally leads into praise for the God who is able to do all this.

What images would you use for who God is for you?

Using the model of Psalm 18, write your own psalm of thanksgiving to God, recounting what he has done for you and who he has been for you before praising and thanking him for his actions and for who he is.

Your heart's desire

Imaginative/going out

Another lesson that Much-Afraid learns on her journey is that when God is having his way, or when she is following his way, then that is the most important thing and nothing else matters but doing as the Shepherd commands. It can be a difficult lesson to learn and may seem impossible. How can doing what someone else wants be a good thing? It is a hard lesson to learn, until you realise that God only wants the best for us.

I remember a period where I was trying to discern what direction my future might take and was taken aback when I was asked, 'What would your dream future look like?' I realised that, until that point, I had assumed that if it was God's path, it would be hard and I wouldn't like it. Seeing it the other way round, and knowing my desire and God's could be the same, was revolutionary.

Much-Afraid learns the lesson of putting aside her will and following the Shepherd in many steps throughout her journey. At each point of learning, she finds or is given a stone. She keeps these as symbols of her learning and reminders of the need for patience as she waits for the Shepherd to give her her heart's desire (which is what he promises her at the start of the journey).

Either imagine walking along an easy path with Jesus, or go out for a walk, imagining Jesus beside you as you walk. Look around you. See the hills in the distance and far-off promises of mountains. Feel the earth beneath your feet and the sunshine on your face. Notice the easy pace with which you cover the ground.

As you walk, tell Jesus about your life, what is important and what is troubling you. Tell him about your hopes and fears for the future.

Then Jesus asks if you are ready to accept whatever he asks you to do. Are you willing to let go of your will and your priorities and follow those of Jesus?

As he asks, notice your inner response. What stops you? What excites you? When you are ready, respond; be honest and be prepared to listen to Jesus as much as you talk to him.

Find or draw something to represent your response and to act as a reminder of what has happened today.

Allow Jesus to walk you back to your home or room and to show his ongoing love for you.

Hannah Hurnard

Spotlight

Hannah Hurnard was born in 1905 in Colchester to Quaker parents. She grew up as a Quaker, though by her teens she had come to dread the meetings, failing to find God and an experience of God as her parents and others seemed to be doing. She hated the Bible and doubted God's existence.

By the age of 19, she had developed a stammer and had considered suicide. Her father took her to a convention in Keswick where she hoped that, if God were real, he would make himself known to her. Alone in her room one evening, she opened her Bible and read the account of Elijah and the prophets of Baal and realised God was asking her to make a sacrifice of her life and to speak out in public. With her stammer, this was the last thing she wanted to do. As her faith grew, her stammer decreased. She went to Israel as a missionary to the Jews and stayed there through the war of independence.

Hinds' Feet on High Places in many ways reflects the author's life as she laid it down for God and explores how she overcame her stammering and shyness as she worked in ways she would previously have found repulsive.

In her later life, she went on to write a number of books which show how far her beliefs moved away from her earlier evangelical roots. Though her later works may not be popular, *Hinds' Feet on High Places* is seen by many as an inspirational book and reflects her sound beliefs at the time.

She died in 1990.

The valley

Intercession

After many trials and travels through the desert and lowlands, often seemingly heading away from the High Places, Much-Afraid does reach the High Places. She is given a new name, Grace and Glory, and her companions, Sorrow and Suffering, are renamed Joy and Peace. But this is not the end; there are still higher places to be explored and new lessons to be learned. Grace and Glory, as she now is, leaps and bounds over the mountain alongside the King.

The book ends when Grace and Glory is taken by the King to a new valley. She walks to the end of the valley and stops to look at the view. There she sees a place that looks vaguely familiar: the Valley of Humiliation where she had grown up and where her relatives still live. She remembers her Aunt Dismal Foreboding, her many cousins and old Lord Fearing, and tears well up and her heart throbs with pain. She no longer sees them all as 'horrible enemies, but now she realised that they were just miserable beings such as she had been herself. They were indwelt and tormented by their different besetting sins and ugly natures, just as she had been by her fears' (p. 154).

She recognises the causes of their wretched lives and knows that the Shepherd could rescue them as he had rescued Much-Afraid, but we read that they are not willing to let the King into their homes or even speak to him, and so the only way is for someone they know to go and speak to them and show them what the King could do. As Grace and Glory and the King prepare to go down into the valley, she sees a waterfall she had passed earlier and now understands the excitement of the water drops in falling over the edge and going down and down to the valley below.

> She was beholding a wondrous and glorious truth; 'a great multitude whom no man could number' brought like herself by the King to the Kingdom of Love and to the High Places so that they could now pour out their lives in gladdest abandonment, leaping down with Him to the sorrowful, desolate places below, to share with others the life which they had received.
>
> p. 157

She recognises that 'he brought me to the heights just for this'.

Grace and Glory, with Joy and Peace, go down with the King singing:

> Make haste, my beloved, and be thou like to a roe or to a young hart upon the mountains of spices.
>
> SONG OF SOLOMON 8:14, KJV

Reflect on some of the darker places you have visited in the past, or where you may be now, and then bring them before the King who can turn Much-Afraid into Grace and Glory.

> God, the Lord, is my strength;
> he makes my feet like the feet of a deer,
> and makes me tread upon the heights.
>
> HABAKKUK 3:19

Living lightly

Sally Welch

No bag for your journey

Introduction

Read Matthew 10:1–10.

The very first pilgrimage I ever took, 20 years ago, led from the town of Assisi to that of Gubbio, towns made famous by their association with St Francis. It wasn't a long journey, but on the long, winding path which led through the green hills of Umbria, I learned lessons which would change my life. It was here, too, that I first discovered St Francis, his passion for life and his passion for living lightly to the things of this world in order to make space for the kingdom. Committed to proclaiming the good news of the gospel to the poor and outcast of society, Francis lived what he preached, sharing all that he had with those he met, caring for the whole of creation, preaching a message of 'living without appropriating'.

Taking his message into my heart, I began my own journey towards living without appropriating, starting with my physical burden of a heavy rucksack, filled with the things which I had thought necessary for my survival. I soon discovered that the less I carried, the easier the journey. I gradually took this into other areas of my life, using the things of the world sparingly, taking only what I needed. I discovered that this attitude also led to a lightness of mind and heart, as I let go of regrets and envy and dropped my burdens of expectation and guilt. Using the words of Jesus to his disciples, we can explore what it means to live without appropriating – to enjoy the things of the world without holding onto them; to leave behind the unnecessary in order to hold more tightly onto our vision of the kingdom.

As a way of preparation, consider what five things would you rescue from your burning house. What do they say about you and your values?

Not even an extra tunic

Reflective

Read Luke 9:1–6.

Jesus' injunctions to his disciples are clear and firm – as they set out to declare God's message to his people, they are not to rely on anything but the word of God for their support. They may not look for comfort in material possessions, nor seek to protect themselves from the trials which may come their way. St Francis took Jesus' message seriously, and allowed himself and his followers no personal possessions, declaring that material wealth obstructed our vision of the kingdom.

Most of us are not able to strip ourselves of our material goods in such a dramatic way, but we can determine that they will not become obstacles to us in our quest for a deeper relationship with God. While we can enjoy God's gifts to us, we must not allow ownership to prevent us from sharing what we have been given with others, nor be frightened to risk what we have for the sake of the kingdom.

Make a list of the 20 things you possess which are the costliest in monetary terms. Study the list – are they useful things or decorative? Do they have another purpose besides their monetary value? Are they the things that are most precious to you personally, or do you hold on to them simply because they are costly? Do they make you feel better about yourself, and if so, how do they do this? How would you feel if they were all taken from you – would you feel as if you had lost a part of yourself or would you feel relieved? Does caring for them bring you joy or are they a burden to you? Consider giving one of them away or selling one and giving the money to a charity.

Leave only footprints

Going out

Read Genesis 2:4–15. 'The Lord God took the man and put him in the garden of Eden to till it and keep it' (v. 15).

'Take only photographs, leave only footprints', we are exhorted by the countryside code, and one of the ways in which we must ensure that we do indeed live lightly is in our relationship to the rest of creation. Given stewardship by God, human beings quickly began to abuse this privilege, exploiting both land and creatures for their own selfish ends. For those of us who are living with the inheritance of this wanton destruction, the necessity of living responsibly on this planet is even more important. More than ever, we must consider the impact each of our actions makes on the wellbeing of the earth and of those who share it with us. It is no longer enough to recycle; we must go one step further in our efforts to reuse or, better still, not to use at all if a more environmentally sympathetic way can be found. In learning to love and understand nature, we gain not only an understanding of God but of ourselves. Concern for the environment, concrete physical action and commitment to caring for our surroundings and our relationship with the creatures that inhabit them must be the physical living out of a belief in the oneness and uniqueness of God's creations.

Take time today to rejoice in the beauty of the landscape which surrounds you, and to improve it in at least one way. This may be as simple as picking up a piece of litter and disposing of it carefully or it may consist of planting seeds for the enjoyment of future generations.

Let the heavens be glad, and let the earth rejoice;
let the sea roar, and all that fills it;
let the field exult, and everything in it.
Then shall all the trees of the forest sing for joy
before the Lord.

PSALM 96:11–13

God's gifts

Creative

Read Matthew 20:1–15. 'Are you envious because I am generous?' (v. 15).

Those poor workers in the vineyard – all day long they have toiled in the harsh heat, under the glare of the sun, looking forward to the time when they can finally stop work and, taking their pay, make their way home to rest. How angry they must have been at those who came afterwards and received the same amount of money for less work! But what a burden those expectations were, spoiling the satisfaction of a good day's work for a fair day's pay. How sad that they allowed the fortune of others to mar their own upright behaviour.

The advent of Facebook and other social media makes the sort of pressure which the vineyard workers experienced even greater nowadays. Everywhere, it seems, there are people who are more fortunate than ourselves, enjoying greater luxury, more success, making our own achievements feel somehow less satisfactory. We must fight against such comparisons, focusing instead on all that has been given to us, asking God for the grace to use our gifts to his purpose.

Find a packet of coloured sweets and tip them out. (If you prefer, you can use small soft fruits or different savoury snacks for the exercise.) Choosing at random, each time you select a green sweet, thank God for an aspect of nature which you appreciate as you slowly suck the sweet. When you pick a red one, think of a gift or skill you have and be thankful; for the orange sweets, pray for a person you love; for a yellow, offer a prayer for your church or community. At the end of your prayer time, ask God for the gift of gratitude and try to carry a sense of thankfulness into the rest of your day.

Wealth or poverty

Creative

Read Matthew 6:19–21. 'For where your treasure is, your heart will be also' (v. 21).

For St Francis, the dangers of wealth were obvious – the more one had, the more time was spent in caring for that wealth. The greater the riches, the more frightened one became at the thought of losing them. Fear makes people selfish and angry, hostile towards those they perceive to be threatening their possessions or trying to take them away. Better by far, he argued, to own nothing, for thus one cannot be afraid of loss.

Greed is an invidious thing – it feeds on itself and destroys those whom it inhabits, gradually taking over until nothing but desire is left. In today's society, we are constantly battered by attempts to make us get more, spend more, buy more, have more – until, unless we are careful, our whole lives can be taken over. We must be on our guard against this, holding before us the abundance that is ours, and sharing what we have with those who have not.

Look through newspapers and magazines for advertisements for luxurious and costly objects and cut them out, or print them from your computer. Stick them on to a large piece of paper at random, overlapping each other until you have a picture of wealth. Then look again, through the news sections this time, for images of people in poverty: refugees, those living in conflict areas or countries suffering from drought. Glue these on top of your images of wealth. Where should our hearts be? Ask God to show you a way to serve those living in poverty and desperation. Keep this picture where you will see it often during the day, as a reminder of the dangers of selfishness.

Losing life

Action

Read Matthew 10:37–39. 'Those who lose their life for my sake will find it' (v. 39).

When I have a writing deadline to meet which I am finding particularly challenging, I tend to do all sorts of other tasks in order to put off actually sitting down at my desk to write. I will sort the laundry, see to the chickens, maybe even cook dinner in advance – anything except get on with the task! When I am really desperate, I take a train journey. There, away from any distractions, forced to focus on the task in hand, the deadline can at last be met.

We all have similar tasks which are necessary but which we prefer to postpone and put off – sadly, this is often the case with prayer. We might be finding it particularly hard going; we might be so busy that it creeps unnoticed down the priority list; we might have got out of the habit for some reason. The art of living lightly consists not merely in freeing ourselves from those material things which block our path to God, but from mental attitudes as well – all must be swept clear so that we can keep the main thing as the main thing: seeking first the kingdom of God and his righteousness.

Make a new beginning by tidying up your prayer space – or by establishing one if you have not done so yet. This does not have to be a large area; it may simply be a comfortable chair with a table beside it to rest a book upon. It could, if you have the space, be a particular place where you can hang pictures or objects as reminders of prayer, or keep significant books, a candle to light or a cross to use as a focal point.

Do not judge

Imaginative

Read Matthew 7:1–5.

Since that first pilgrimage through Italy, I have made many more – in England and in Europe, on my own and in the company of others. Each has taught me many things, but perhaps I learn most when I travel in the company of other people. For there I learn not just about myself but about others – more specifically, I learn about myself in relation to others. The most humbling lesson I have learnt is my quickness to judge others on first impressions – which are not as revealing as tradition has it! So many times, I have made assumptions about another's nature or character only to have these fall away in the light of conversations and discussions. Hidden depths have been revealed: a broadness of experience perhaps, or a gift or skill that is not immediately apparent on initial encounters; a joy for living in the face of serious challenges; a sadness which has been overcome.

Next time you meet someone new, instead of examining their faces or clothing for clues as to who they are and what position they hold in society, why not look at their shoes? Imagine the distance these shoes have travelled, think how their footsteps have been heavy with grief and sorrow or light-hearted with joy. Picture them running to meet someone they love or saying goodbye, perhaps for the last time. Notice the distortions caused by wear and consider the effect life experiences have had on their character. Pray for the wearer, and ask God for the grace to see them through his eyes, as one of his children. You might undertake this exercise with the shoes of those who share your house, or with your own, witnesses as they are of journeys undertaken and paths trodden.

Seventy times seven

Creative

Read Matthew 18:21–22.

Poor Peter! He knows, as do all human beings, how hard it is to forgive people who have hurt you. But he wants to follow Jesus and accepts that to be a disciple will involve some challenges. But surely there is a limit to what he is being asked to do? Surely he cannot be expected to forgive someone again and again? But that is what Jesus requires of him and of us all. In order to live lightly, we must put down not only the physical objects which slow us and hinder our journey, but those habits of thinking that drag us back into the past to ponder past injuries, keeping them alive and in the present, spreading their poison. Forgiving those who have offended against us will not change the events of the past, but it will change our ability to move forward into the future.

Find a whiteboard or a chalkboard, a patch of sand or earth or even a mirror which you can steam up – anything that you can write on and wipe off. Spend some time thinking of those people who have hurt you and who you are finding it hard to forgive. Write their names down. Consider how your grievances and hurts have affected your life and how much damage they have done. Pray the Lord's prayer slowly and carefully, then say each name followed by 'I forgive you, for Jesus' sake.' This exercise can be quite painful and challenging and you may need to repeat it a number of times.

> Whenever you stand praying, forgive, if you have anything against anyone.
>
> Mark 11:25

Forgiving ourselves

Creative

Read Matthew 26:26–29. 'For this is my blood of the covenant, which is poured out for many for the forgiveness of sins' (v. 28).

People react in a number of different ways when I tell them I work as a parish priest. A few people end the conversation immediately and walk away, but not many. Some immediately offer their religious credentials, detailing their responsibilities within their home church and the challenges they face within it. Others offer their opinions on just exactly where the Church of England has gone wrong, sometimes offering suggestions as to how to put it right, sometimes stating that the whole institution should be closed down. Occasionally, however, a person will fall silent. Then they will say to me – 'I would like to go to church, but I have done too many things wrong. It's not the place for a sinner like me.' My response to this is always – the church is exactly the right place for you! It's only for sinners!

If we find forgiving others challenging, it can be many times harder forgiving ourselves. How many times have we looked back with regret at our words and actions, wished we had made different decisions or followed different paths? Then we must remind ourselves of the essence of Jesus' ministry – that he came to save the lost and that forgiveness is available for all who ask for it.

Find a water-soluble pen and write on your hands (and arms if necessary) the events and actions for which you seek forgiveness. Under running water, wash your hands clean, thanking God.

> But you were washed, you were sanctified, you were justified in the name of the Lord Jesus Christ and in the Spirit of our God.
>
> 1 Corinthians 6:11

Do not worry

Meditative

Read Matthew 6:25–34. 'So do not worry about tomorrow, for tomorrow will bring worries of its own' (v. 34).

How many times have we heard or read this passage, with its references to the beauty of creation and the great love the Father has for everything he has created. With what earnestness does Jesus tell us not to allow ourselves to be diverted from our journey forward by constantly looking back! We have been offered the gift of forgiveness, the opportunity to lay our burden of sin at the foot of the cross, enabling us to walk on more freely, rejoicing in the landscape that surrounds us. We are encouraged not to worry about what the future holds, because it is being held by God, but to think instead of how we might serve God in the present.

'Now we are children of God,' we are told in 1 John 3:2 (NIV), and it is only in the now that we are truly alive. We must let go of the past and be confident that, whatever is in the future, we do not face it alone but in the company of one who loves us.

Take a moment to be aware of the breath moving in and out of your body. Feel how it fills your lungs, bringing life and energy. Focus on the breath as it moves in and out. If your mind wanders, do not become anxious or concerned; simply take notice and return to the breath, in and out. During the day, take time to stop and breathe, relishing the moment, feeling the love and life of God within it.

> Let this presence settle into your bones, and allow your soul
> the freedom to sing, dance, praise and love.
>
> St Teresa of Avila

Transformed into beauty

Reflective

Read 2 Corinthians 12:1–10. 'Therefore I am content with weaknesses, insults, hardships, persecutions, and calamities for the sake of Christ; for whenever I am weak, then I am strong' (v. 10).

When exploring the practice of living lightly, we can consider both physical and mental burdens and reflect on the way in which each one can hinder us on our journey into a deeper relationship with God. We can find ways in which these burdens can be minimised or laid down, trusting in Christ as our guide and companion as we move forward.

However, there are some burdens which cannot be put aside, which we must carry with us, despite our reluctance to do so. These can be physical disabilities or long-term illness; they can be the necessity of caring for an older or younger member of the family. Mental and emotional burdens can also be our journey companions: memories of events which cannot be removed, psychological damage which remains with us despite our best efforts. Paul writes movingly of his own 'thorn' – the subject of much speculation by Bible critics. We do not need to know what this was; it is enough that it caused him 'torment'. In our turn, it is sufficient that we acknowledge our burdens and seek to find strength to bear them in God's love and good purposes for us: 'My grace is sufficient for you, for power is made perfect in weakness' (v. 9).

Kintsugi is the Japanese art of mending broken pots with lacquer mixed with gold or silver, giving the repaired object beautiful golden seams. The broken object thus becomes not something to be thrown away but more precious than before. So too can our damage and hurt be transformed into beauty as we help others by our experiences and wisdom.

Reflecting on the map

Creative

Read Jeremiah 29:11–14. 'When you search for me, you will find me; if you seek me with all your heart' (v. 13).

For my husband, the best bit of the journey is not the actual activity itself but the planning. For weeks before a pilgrimage, the dining room table will be covered with maps as he studies routes, works out the best places to stop and rest, and decides which sites should be visited on the route. After the journey, he will take out those same maps and read them the way others read their journals, remembering the places and events and fixing them in his mind.

So too our life journeys can be seen as a map of our route towards the heavenly city, with Christ as both our journey and our destination. We will encounter dangers and sorrows on the way, as surely as there will be joys and triumphs, each fixing themselves in our hearts and on our minds. If we travel lightly, trusting in God to supply our needs, sharing what we have with our companions, supporting each other in times of difficulty, our journey will be so much easier, and it will be seen that our destination lies within us as well as beyond.

Draw a map of the area or countries in which you have lived. It does not need to be to scale, but simply to include all those places you have called home. Reflect on the lessons which you have learnt in each location, the people you met, the events you lived through. Try and discern God's actions in all those places and give thanks for the richness and depth of your experiences. Pray for an awareness of his presence as you continue your journey.

Our heart is restless until it rests in you.

St Augustine of Hippo

Grateful

Dorinda Miller

Great

Introduction

To be grateful, to be thankful, to have an attitude of gratitude is not only a positive way of being, but it also flows from an awareness of all we have received from God. Aware of the blessings he has bestowed upon us through our acceptance of the gift of abundant life (John 10:10), our commitment is to follow him.

In *The Times* newspaper, in the Mind Games section, is the Polygon. The task is to make as many words as possible out of the available letters. This series will adopt the idea, and will make twelve words from 'Grateful': Great, Grate, Rate, Late, Gruel, Raft, Graft, Fault, Tear, Gear, Fear and Tuft (if we 'cheat' and use the 't' twice). We will consider each one in turn.

As we read and study the Bible, we can gain an understanding of the greatness of God through the characters and events that are recorded in it. As we continue the journey of faith within our churches, communities and the individuals we are close to, who are travelling the Way with us, we will have our own stories and testimonies as to how great God is and how great are his love, mercy, compassion for us.

Take a few moments to reflect on how you have seen God's greatness in action recently (e.g. in your own life, or in a book, or in a sermon or podcast).

Now read the following three verses slowly, three times, and then choose one of them. Turn your chosen verse over and over in your mind and listen to what God will share with you through it.

But may all who search for you
  be filled with joy and gladness in you.
May those who love your salvation
  repeatedly shout, 'God is great!'

PSALM 70:4

For you are great and perform wonderful deeds.
  You alone are God.

PSALM 86:10

Great is the Lord! He is most worthy of praise!

PSALM 96:4

Grate

Imaginative

As well as being used to describe the metal bars and framework that we place wood or coal on in a fireplace, or the action with a grater to shred some foods, the word 'grate' also means to irritate or annoy.

Travelling through life, we do from time to time come across people and situations which do indeed grate with us. We find that the 'ful' disappears from grateful and we are left with irritation and annoyance!

In 2 Kings 5, we read the story of Naaman, the commander of the king of Aram's army. He had leprosy, but his wife's Israelite maid explained that he could be cured if he went to see God's prophet in Samaria. He duly went and was most put out when the prophet Elisha did not greet him personally and sent a messenger to tell him to wash seven times in the River Jordan. The instruction grated with him. It was not what he had expected and it prompted him to go away in a rage.

However, his servant encouraged him to go to the Jordan and wash seven times as instructed. When he did so, he was healed. He then returned to Elisha and acknowledged the God of Israel.

Read 2 Kings 5:9–14 a couple of times and then imagine your way through it, in whichever way seems best for you. You may like to be Naaman or you may prefer to watch the story unfold as if you were watching a film.

As you entered into the story, what thoughts or feelings emerged? Is there anything which is currently affecting you physically or emotionally that you would like God to wash away from you? In the stillness, speak to God about this. Finally, read these verses from Psalm 103:2–5.

> Let all that I am praise the Lord;
> may I never forget the good things he does for me.
> He forgives all my sins
> and heals all my diseases.
> He redeems me from death
> and crowns me with love and tender mercies.
> He fills my life with good things.

Rate

Meditative

To some people, life appears to be passing by at an alarming rate! To others, the rate seems slower. With roles and responsibilities to carry out and the constant bombardment of communications from a variety of sources, it can be a challenge to slow down, to stop and be grateful for God's provision for us.

One way that has had a positive effect on enabling me to slow down and reflect on the events of the day with gratitude has been the Examen. You might be familiar with this exercise, which was described by St Ignatius of Loyola as part of his Spiritual Exercises. It is in essence a five-step exercise and is well documented and described (see **www.ignatianspirituality.com/ignatian-prayer/the-examen**). However, I have found Ian Adams' take on it particularly helpful as he incorporates gestures into the steps (*Running Over Rocks* by Ian Adams, Canterbury Press Norwich, 2013, p. 98).

- Be still and become aware of the presence of God. (*Open your hands.*)
- Review the events of the day with gratitude. (*Place your hands on your heart.*)
- Recall the emotions you have experienced during the day, and consider why you felt this way. (*Place your hands on your stomach.*)
- Select one moment/element of the day and pray about it. (*Hands to lips.*)
- Look forward to tomorrow. (*Open your hands again.*)

I invite you to pray the Examen daily as you explore gratefulness.

Late

Reflective

As the White Rabbit said, in Lewis Carroll's *Alice in Wonderland*, 'I'm late, I'm late. For a very important date. No time to say Hello, Goodbye. I'm late, I'm late, I'm late.' Do you find yourself on time? Out of time? Running late? What is your relationship with time and punctuality in this season of your life? Do you find yourself with too much time on your hands or not enough time to get through the daily schedule of tasks/activities and responsibilities? While we might keep an eye on the time, Ecclesiastes 3 tells us that there is time for everything under the sun.

I have certainly found on countless occasions over the years that God has stretched out the time and enabled me to do more than I thought was possible within the allotted time frame. As the Psalmist said, ‘My times are in your hands’ (Psalm 31:15, NIV). The key to this, in my experience, is keeping to the time I have set apart to be with the Lord, before rushing headlong into a busy schedule.

Take a few moments to settle into stillness, in whichever way seems most appropriate for you today, and then take time to reflect on being late. Are you ever late for events or appointments? How does this make you feel? How does it make those you are meeting feel? Is being late a conscious or unconscious strategy? Or is it just a vagary of the transport system?

After reflecting, listen to the Lord and seek his perspective on this for you.

Then pray through the insights you have gained and echo the words of Psalm 31:15 above, with gratitude.

Gruel

Bible reading

In the story of *Oliver Twist* by Charles Dickens, the young Oliver, who is poorly fed in the workhouse where he lives, famously asks Mr Bumble the parish beadle, ‘Please sir, I want some more.’ His request for more gruel, a thin porridge of oats and milk or water, causes uproar.

Hunger continues to be a persistent issue in many parts of the world today, even though the world does produce enough food to feed everyone. Natural disasters, poverty, famine, drought and conflicts/wars are among the contributing factors to this inequality of food distribution.

In Mark 6:30–44, read the account of Jesus feeding the 5,000.

As it was getting late in the day, the disciples suggest to Jesus that he send the people away so they can get food. Jesus tells them to feed the people, and they find five loaves and two fish and bring them to him. He gives thanks, breaks the loaves and the food is distributed to all present and they all have enough. Furthermore, twelve baskets of leftovers are collected.

Two significant themes in this account are giving and thanksgiving. The food was given to the disciples, who in turn gave it to Jesus, who with thanksgiving broke the loaves, and the food was given to the people.

Reflect on this account in Mark 6:30–44. Then pray for provision for those who are in need. Ask the Lord if there is any practical action he would have you take in this respect. Then close with thanksgiving for all that you have access to.

Raft

Creative

While we do not often find ourselves at sea on a life raft, we can be grateful that should we encounter difficulties in the sea around the UK, the Republic of Ireland, the Channel Islands and the Isle of Man, the Royal National Lifeboat Institution can come to our rescue.

As we journey through life, there are times when people, events and situations can make us feel as though we are facing a storm or waves or that we are traversing choppy water. What structures, strategies, social networks do you have in place, in your life, to act as a life raft in times of trouble and trauma?

Recall a time when you experienced trouble, difficulty or trauma. Draw a life raft and write on the planks of the raft the people, places, communities and organisations that helped you negotiate your way through the rough sea to a more peaceful stretch of water.

When you have completed your raft, consider what else might have been helpful to you at that time and write those things on planks, adding them to the raft. Are there any steps you can take to ensure that you have all you need in place, to help you chart troubled waters in the future?

Now reflect on God's provision for you and take a moment or two to pray with thanksgiving and gratitude. Read Psalm 100 (NIV):

Shout for joy to the Lord, all the earth.
Worship the Lord with gladness;
come before him with joyful songs.
Know that the Lord is God.
It is he who made us, and we are his;
we are his people, the sheep of his pasture.

Enter his gates with thanksgiving
and his courts with praise;
give thanks to him and praise his name.
For the Lord is good and his love endures for ever;
his faithfulness continues through all generations.

Graft

Reflective

To the medics among us, 'graft' will refer to removing a healthy piece of body tissue and using it to repair a part of the body that is damaged. To the gardeners among us, 'graft' will refer to the insertion of a twig or shoot into a tree trunk or stem of another plant. To many of us, the phrase 'hard graft' will refer to working hard.

Work is an integral part of life for adults and, in many parts of the world, for children too. In his book *Aging Matters* (Eerdmans Publishing Company, 2016, pp. 20–23), R. Paul Stevens suggests the following reasons for work:

- We are made to work
- Work is good for the world
- Work is good for us
- Work can be a practical way to love our neighbours
- Work participates in spreading the kingdom of God
- Work prepares us for the life to come.

Take a few moments to recall your own work history; remember the highlights as well as the more challenging aspects. Read the verses below and then turn your recollections and thoughts about work into prayer with gratitude for the gift of work, in whichever form you have experienced it.

> Use your hands for good hard work, and then give generously to others in need.
>
> EPHESIANS 4:28

> We were not idle when we were with you. We never accepted food from anyone without paying for it. We worked hard day and night so we would not be a burden to any of you. We certainly had the right to ask you to feed us, but we wanted to give you an example to follow. Even while we were with you, we gave you this command: 'Those unwilling to work will not get to eat.'
>
> 2 THESSALONIANS 3:7–10

> Even so, I have noticed one thing, at least, that is good. It is good for people to eat, drink, and enjoy their work under the sun during the short life God has given them, and to accept their lot in life... To enjoy your work and accept your lot in life – this is indeed a gift from God.
>
> ECCLESIASTES 5:18–19

Fault

Reflective

Whether by failing or through a flaw, or by mistake or misdeed, or through error or offence, we are all, at times, at fault. Thankfully, God will not love us any more or less as a result of our behaviour and we can be grateful that we are each a work in progress, as he carries out his transformative work in us.

As David noted in Psalm 19:12 (NIV), 'But who can discern their own errors? Forgive my hidden faults.'

The apostle Paul, in his letter to Timothy, offers some advice on how to live. Read the following verses slowly three times and make a note of which verses are highlighted for you today.

> But you, Timothy, are a man of God; so run from all these evil things. Pursue righteousness and a godly life, along with faith, love, perseverance, and gentleness. Fight the good fight for the true faith. Hold tightly to the eternal life to which God has called you, which you have declared so well before many witnesses. And I charge you before God, who gives life to all, and before Christ Jesus, who gave a good testimony before Pontius Pilate, that you obey this command without wavering. Then no one can find fault with you from now until our Lord Jesus Christ comes again.
>
> 1 TIMOTHY 6:11–14

Now choose a phrase or verse and spend a few minutes with it. Turn it over and over in your mind, let it sink into your heart and listen to what God wants to say to you through it.

Read the verse below, from the letter of Jude, before ending with prayer and gratefulness for what you have received from God during this time of reflection.

> Now all glory to God, who is able to keep you from falling away and will bring you with great joy into his glorious presence without a single fault.
>
> JUDE 24

Tear

Imaginative

We can find ourselves in tears, in floods of tears, bursting into tears and close to tears as a result of a variety of situations. The ability to shed a tear (or two, or more!) aids our expression of feelings and emotions that may not easily be put into words. They are a language of their own and we can be grateful for them, even if we are challenged by the situation that prompted them to flow.

Two Bible passages that illustrate these points are the story of Hannah, in 1 Samuel 1:1–20, and the story of the woman with the alabaster jar of perfume in Luke 7:36–50. Read these accounts and then choose one of them.

Read the one you have chosen again, slowly, and then take a moment or two to become still. You may like to take a deep breath in and to let it out slowly a few times as you let go of the things on your mind and move into a place of peace and stillness.

In your imagination, enter into the story you have chosen either as Hannah, the woman or as an observer. Notice as many details as you can about the setting, watch the scene unfold, see Hannah/the woman, observe her actions, enter into her feelings. Notice the other people in the story, their reaction to the event. Listen to the words of Eli/Jesus, watch Hannah/the woman respond. As an observer, does Eli/Jesus have any words of wisdom for you and your situation?

As the scene comes to a close, rest in the stillness and then express your gratitude to God for what you have received through this time of meditation.

You may like to record your insights and thoughts in your journal.

Finally, we can be encouraged, too, by the words of Psalm 56:8, which tell us that God has 'collected all my tears in your bottle. You have recorded each one in your book.'

Gear

Litany

In the same way that vehicles have gears to accommodate the varying speeds they travel at, so we too need to adjust our pace of life from time to time in order to keep travelling along the road of life. Sometimes we need to step up a gear for a season and sometimes we need to step down a gear. Sometimes we find that 'traffic jams', 'road blocks' and 'traffic incidents' force us to move in a way or at a speed that we had not intended. They say that 'variety is the spice of life' and as far as is possible, we do well to embrace the variety with a grateful heart.

In *An Ignatian Book of Days* (Loyola Press, 2014, p. 117), Jim Manney includes a Litany of Gratitude. He suggests beginning with an awareness of God's presence and then asking God for an awareness of all the gifts God has given you over the course of your life and also to ask for a spirit of gratitude.

The Litany begins with thanksgiving for creation before moving on to be grateful for parents, family, ourselves and our physical faculties, our attributes and talents, our friends, work, play, possessions, ending with 'Your time to live, no matter how quickly it seems to pass.'

I invite you to pray this Litany or to write your own, and to pray it every day for the next few days.

Fear

Spotlight

There are between 230 and 500 verses relating to fear in the Bible, depending on which version you use. There are notably more in the Old Testament than in the New Testament.

While it is neither advisable nor healthy to live our lives in constant fear, there are times and occasions when we do experience fear, either briefly or over a longer period.

When I lived overseas, there were occasions when I experienced fear due to political unrest. I have found myself unexpectedly facing mobs and demonstrations and, on one occasion, I found myself, with my children, stuck in our car on a railway crossing, with a train approaching in one direction and a riotous mob in the other! I am so grateful to God for the ways in which he enabled me to emerge from these encounters unscathed.

On another occasion, we were burgled during the night when I was at home alone with my young children. I woke to hear the door of my bedroom bang and when no child appeared at my bedside, I went to investigate. On entering the sitting room, I discovered the veranda door was wide open and all the cupboard doors were open too. My heart missed a beat and, having locked the veranda door, I went at once to check on the children. They were both sleeping soundly. I then realised that I might have locked the intruders in the property, so I checked every room. In doing so, my son woke up and asked what was happening. He joined me in the search and thankfully we did not find anyone. He returned to bed and, having prayed for him, I went into the sitting room, where I suddenly felt overwhelmed by the situation and fearful, although God had given me peace until that point. I tried to ring some friends, but understandably they did not answer their phone, since it was around 3.00 am!

As I stood beside the phone, I found myself thinking that rather than remain fearful and shaken, now was definitely the moment to pick up a mustard seed of faith and pray for peace, protection and a good night's sleep. As I began to pray, these words came instantly to my mind: 'In peace I will lie down and sleep, for you alone, O Lord, will keep me safe' (Psalm 4:8). Fear departed and I did indeed sleep soundly for the rest of the night.

Tuft

Creative

When austerity began to hit my local Borough Council a few years ago, one of the first things to be curtailed was mowing the grass in the park at the bottom of my garden.

It used to be mown with unfailing regularity all summer. Now they just cut some wide paths through the grass and let the rest grow. The result is a meadow with tall grass and buttercups! Towards the end of summer, the grass naturally withers and dies, as do the flowers, leaving a few tufts or clumps of green grass.

I invite you to draw a meadow (no A-level art required for this!) with some tufts of grass scattered on it. When you have done so, consider: What are the 'tufts' in your life? i.e. the things which remain and are constant (faith, family, friends, etc.). When you have written these on your tufts, read the verses below and express your gratefulness to God for what he has placed in your life.

> Oh, how grateful and thankful I am to the Lord because he is so good. I will sing praise to the name of the Lord who is above all lords.
>
> PSALM 7:17, TLB

> Accept my grateful thanks and teach me your desires.
>
> PSALM 119:108, TLB

In his letter to the Romans, the apostle Paul reminds them that they are part of God's kingdom because they believe in God, and he encourages them to be humble and grateful. As this series comes to a close, let us take his advice:

> Watch out! Remember that those branches, the Jews, were broken off because they didn't believe God, and you are there only because you do. Do not be proud; be humble and grateful – and careful.
>
> ROMANS 11:20, TLB

Winter food for thought

Janet Lunt

Winter darkness

Introduction/creative

We are very familiar with the concept of *desert* or *wilderness* symbolising periods on the Christian journey of searching, thirsting for God's presence and the intentional paring down of comfort to help focus on God, such as during Lent. Similarly, *winter* can lend symbolic understanding to states on the spiritual journey, so this will be our springboard for thought and prayer over the next fortnight.

In the northern hemisphere, the first striking image that signals the approach of winter is darkness. It closes in, shortening the day. The lack of sunlight lessens our supply of vitamin D, and we resort to hours of artificial lighting. This lack can make us long for spring, or holidays in sunnier climes.

Find a space in the darkness of early morning or evening, and imagine living without electricity or gas, with just firelight or candlelight to lengthen your day. How different would your life be? How would your productivity change? How might it feel to live with the natural rhythm of our turning planet?

Light a candle and spend time thinking about the blessing of light in all its forms, particularly the sun. Consider, too, the blessing of night.

In Britain's past, Celtic Christians lived more closely with nature and seasonal rhythms than we do today. Use my Celtic-style prayer below asking for God's blessing, or write your own Blessing of Light. It could begin with: 'Bless to me, O God…'

Your blessing of light be upon me this season,
O Heaven-light shining, around and within,
igniting my heart like a great Winter fire,
for warming the stranger, my friend and my kin.
Your blessing of light be upon me this season,
O Heaven-light shining by day and by night,
be guiding my steps on the winding and narrow,
my soul kept in safety from harm and from fright.

In the dark

Bible reading

In the Bible, there are different uses of the word 'darkness': descriptions of the benign, natural darkness of night, and innumerably more instances representing such states as spiritual blindness; the unknown; being without God through ignorance or sin. Read through the selection of verses below, noticing different representations of darkness.

You, Lord, keep my lamp burning;
  my God turns my darkness into light.

PSALM 18:28

As a shepherd looks after his scattered flock when he is with them, so will I look after my sheep. I will rescue them from all the places where they were scattered on a day of clouds and darkness.

EZEKIEL 34:12

If I say, 'Surely the darkness will hide me
  and the light become night around me,'
even the darkness will not be dark to you;

> the night will shine like the day,
> for darkness is as light to you.
>
> PSALM 139:11–12

> He reveals deep and hidden things;
> he knows what lies in darkness,
> and light dwells with him.
>
> DANIEL 2:22

> The Lord my God will come, and all the holy ones with him. On that day there will be neither sunlight nor cold, frosty darkness. It will be a unique day – a day known only to the Lord – with no distinction between day and night. When evening comes, there will be light.
>
> ZECHARIAH 14:5–7

> The light shines in the darkness, and the darkness has not overcome it.
>
> JOHN 1:5

> Your eye is the lamp of your body. When your eyes are healthy, your whole body also is full of light. But when they are unhealthy, your body also is full of darkness. See to it, then, that the light within you is not darkness.
>
> LUKE 11:34–35

> For God, who said, 'Let light shine out of darkness,' made his light shine in our hearts to give us the light of the knowledge of God's glory displayed in the face of Christ.
>
> 2 CORINTHIANS 4:6

Darkness is the absence of, and contrast for, light. How would you define the light of God (e.g. righteousness/revelation)? Meditate on one of the verses. Read it several times. Reflect on its meaning. Ask God to speak to you through it. Respond by singing or listening to a hymn or song about light, e.g. the Taizé chant: 'By night we hasten in darkness.'

Arctic beauty

Creative

It was an extraordinary experience visiting northern Finland. The plane landed at night on compacted snow, just within the Arctic Circle. It was minus 20 degrees outside. A three-hour coach ride took us further north to our destination. The next morning, our cosy log cabin opened on to a stunning landscape and the cleanness of the snow was exhilarating.

To survive outside, we had to wear thermal underwear and special outer clothing. Exploring, we found a café on a hilltop so frosted up from exposure that it looked long-deserted, yet inside was a huge log fire and hot food. We travelled through whitened woodland by reindeer-sleigh; Laplanders told us their story; fidgety huskies waited eagerly to transport customers. Just once, we saw a shy red squirrel bound across the surface of deep snow – its frame so light that it left the shallowest of indentations; and joyously, on our last night, green, snaking ribbons of Northern Lights curled slowly and mysteriously overhead. What a Maker! The whole experience was wonder-filled.

My most treasured memory was of a gentle snowfall backlit by low sun that caused individual flakes to sparkle as they fell – a phenomenon known as 'diamond dust'. Looking closely at the newly piled snow, I could make out each flake's unique pattern (Arctic snow being 'dry', so falling in separate flakes).

Find images of snowflakes. Wonder at their fragility and uniqueness. Make a paper snowflake, so delicate that it needs great care to unfold (for example, try searching for 'Instructables How to make six-sided paper snowflakes'). As you open it out, what does it say about your uniqueness as a child of God?

Read Psalm 148, responding to the Great Designer.

For a contemplative experience, watch a short preview of *All Aboard! The Sleigh Ride* on YouTube. The original two-hour BBC4 documentary followed travelling Sami women, their reindeer and cargo, in real-time, with no music or commentary, just natural sounds.

White as snow

Liturgy

When it snows, both countryside and urban landscape are transformed into a picture postcard. Freshly fallen snow is a great equaliser and beautifier. It reminds us of purity, and Isaiah 1:18 aptly uses this imagery:

> 'Come now, let us settle the matter,'
> says the Lord.
> 'Though your sins are like scarlet,
> they shall be as white as snow.'

During Isaiah's vision of being in God's presence, he experienced such great majesty, awe and holiness that he cried out: 'Woe is me! I am lost, for I am a man of unclean lips, and I live among a people of unclean lips' (Isaiah 6:5, NRSV). An angel cleansed his lips with a burning coal, then Isaiah was commissioned to be God's mouthpiece to his people, to speak out against sin, corruption and deserting God. In chapter 1, God addresses an ungrateful, rebellious people over the hypocrisy of their worship and prayer; he cannot bear to hear them because they have blood on their hands. They are told to give up their ways, and seek to be clean. Then, God offers the solution, in verse 18, as above.

God's presence is surrounded by angelic host. Reflect on your experience of God's holiness… and mercy. It is good to examine the heart before making an offering. Consider what may need confessing. Then, sitting or kneeling with your hands palms-upwards, speak your confession to the Lord, using your own words or the ones below. After your prayer, imagine an angel touching your lips with burning coal.

Great and holy Lord,
without you, I am lost;
without your touch, my lips and actions remain unclean.
I confess that my words and worship
have not always pleased your ears.
In your mercy, forgive, cleanse and restore me.
Let your love cover my sins as snow silently covers the land,
and help me cover the sins of others.
Envision me to do justice in faithfulness to your word,
Through Jesus Christ.
Amen

Winter of the soul

Reflective

What gets us through bleak times of the soul, when our prayer seems like breath that freezes as it meets the air? Do we have things, people, places we can turn to that will buoy us up?

'Winter Stores' is a poem by Charlotte Brontë about life. It uses seasonal metaphor to describe times of the 'sunshine of the heart' when sorrow stays away and 'existence seems a summer eve'. However, because time doesn't distinguish between clear or clouded skies, grief or bliss, Brontë considers what the soul extracts from the good times to aid 'winter gloom and scarcity'. Her answer lies in the unseen work of memory toiling like a nectar-seeking bee from flower to flower:

> *'Tis she that from each transient pleasure extracts a lasting good;*
> *'Tis she that finds, in summer, treasure to serve for winter's food.*

If ever a biblical figure has gone through a winter of the soul, it is Job of the Old Testament, a prayerful man whom God allows, for a season, to be afflicted with extreme suffering: loss of family, possessions and health, exacerbated by unhelpful advice from friends. God seems far away, yet Job attempts to accept his lot, and continues to pray.

> God has made me a byword to everyone,
> a man in whose face people spit.
> My eyes have grown dim with grief;
> my whole frame is but a shadow...
> My days have passed, my plans are shattered.
> Yet the desires of my heart
> turn night into day;
> in the face of the darkness light is near.
>
> JOB 17:6–7, 11–12

What enables Job to hang on to faith? Perhaps his prayer habit or past experiences of God comfort him. What do you think the desires of Job's heart might be that 'turn night into day' (v. 12)?

On cold, bitter days of the soul, when God seems far away, prayer unanswered and inspiration frozen, what 'nectar' do you turn to? It might be familiar books, looking back on a prayer diary, a retreat house or encouraging friends of faith. Give some thought to this and to what you could squirrel away, e.g. keeping a prayer journal or collecting scripture promises. Read two sustaining promises in John 16:20–22 and Jeremiah 29:11.

Waiting for spring

Reflective

Winter in the northern hemisphere can present a stark, sometimes grim face – bare landscapes, skeletal trees, dead nature and endless greyness. To survive winter, some creatures hibernate. The deciduous tree goes into a dormant state when everything slows down inside; yet even as it rests, the sap still circulates unseen, and the roots continue to grow – unless the winter is particularly savage. Other plants shrink back to corms or bulbs where underground miracles are wrought.

What can be learned from these processes? Chew on a selection from the following springboards for prayer:

- In secret: Ponder nature's time of slow activity, a necessary part of the season cycle, which happens out of sight – below ground, inside living entities, in darkness. How does this relate to spiritual life? Allow hidden seeds and bulbs to teach you. Plan to plant some bulbs.

- Early signs: In anticipation of early flowers that break through against the odds – modest yet resilient snowdrops and crocuses – look for signs of God at work in the modest and small.

- Bareness: The stark silhouette of a bare tree reveals its complex structure. What are you made of, what strengths remain, if you are stripped of activity and abundance?

- Waiting: You might think about Israel's extremely long wait for their Messiah; or that difficult period for the disciples between Christ's crucifixion and the 'springtime' of meeting the risen Jesus.

- Anticipation: Spend time with Romans 8:20–25, as you await the renewal of all.

Grief like winter

Imaginative

Put yourself imaginatively into the following story, based on John 19:38–42:

Today, I feel so cold inside it may as well be winter. Yesterday was the worst day of my life, of many lives. We watched Jesus of Nazareth die in agony, crying out to God. The sun was eclipsed in sympathy, and a storm broke – a sign from heaven!

I did a daring thing yesterday, for which I may yet pay: I asked Pilate if I could bury the body of Jesus. You see I – Joseph of Arimathea – am a member of the Sanhedrin Council where my fellow elders voted to be rid of Jesus. They will not be happy with me. Recently, I became a disciple of Jesus, as did Nicodemus (also a Council member), although we keep this quiet. The latest meetings have been distressing, as the two of us believe Jesus is the awaited Messiah.

Pilate gladly handed over the deceased, after I explained that my own newly-cut family tomb stood nearby. Jesus, who brought healing to so many, deserved a decent burial, not a criminal's interment. (When my time comes, I will gladly share the grave with my Lord!)

We had to hurry – sabbath approached. Nicodemus and I arranged to meet at Golgotha; he brought myrrh and aloes and I purchased linen. We wanted to bury Jesus properly, according to our customs.

The women followed, those who stayed with him to the end. A sympathetic centurion helped us take him down from the scaffold. How we wept as we bound his cold, stiff body in the linen with the spices. We carried him to the tomb, and laid him gently on the cold stone as if it might hurt his back, still raw from flogging. As we closed the entrance, we wept again, and I remembered his last words, 'It is finished!' Night had fallen, and a chill set in.

I'm not entirely sure what Jesus meant by resurrection. I know the love he kindled in us won't die, and that we will see him again on the last day. But where do we now place our hope for the future of our people in this occupied land, where Rome is brutal and the Sanhedrin blind? And what next for me? I am a changed man. How can I carry on at the Council?

I am cold inside, and cannot stop shivering. The sorrowful scent of myrrh lingers, and grief grips me.

Always winter and never Christmas

Story

Winter metaphor has not been lost on storytellers of the northern hemisphere. I recollect two well-known stories that share a theme of persistent winter. *The Lion, the Witch and the Wardrobe* by C.S. Lewis is the first. The White Witch rules with icy power, her very presence sourcing perpetual winter. It is the allegorical story of four children who pass through a wardrobe into Narnia, its frozen state of tyranny causing an inhabitant to describe it as 'always winter and never Christmas' (ch. 2). The hope of freedom rests with a saviour, the Christ-like lion Aslan, bringer of spring.

The second tale describes persistent winter through an ungenerous, self-protective spirit. *The Selfish Giant*, in the story by Oscar Wilde, finds that spring has bypassed his garden, and eventually discovers the cause is the garden wall he has built to keep the children out. A visit from the Christ-child (whose presence sparks spring) enables the giant to recognise his own selfishness, and to learn that love and generosity drive out perpetual winter. The children could represent anything that God brings into our lives; will we welcome and be blessed, or reject?

A longer story bursting with analogies is the classic tale of *The Snow Queen* by Hans Christian Andersen. We hear of a boy, Kai, who is kidnapped by the evil Queen, and whose heart is saved from being completely frozen for eternity by the love and determination of his friend, Gerda. There are many rich threads that can be drawn out of the tale, not least from Gerda's long journey to find her friend: along the way she is waylaid, sidetracked and kidnapped. Yet, aid always comes to her from somewhere, and when an evil army of ice sentinels try to attack, it is the Lord's Prayer that saves her. A Finnish woman, asked to create a potion to help Gerda overcome the Queen, replies: 'I can give her no greater power than she has already… which consists in her own purity and innocence of heart.' Gerda's determination, faith and love keep her true to her quest.

Try to find one these stories to read, perhaps online (in the case of C.S. Lewis' story, you could read a synopsis). Allow the rich wintry images to speak of the Christian journey. Pray for situations burdened by a long 'winter', without the light relief of Christmas.

Symbolism of the seasons

Poetry/creative

> *How like a winter hath my absence been…*
> *What freezings have I felt, what dark days seen!*
> William Shakespeare, Sonnet 97

Poetry and song often employ seasons symbolically to aid expression. Simon and Garfunkel sing of 'A Hazy Shade of Winter' to describe regret over an ended relationship; in the hit-song 'September-November', Frank Sinatra laments life running out of time as it moves towards the year's end.

Haiku is a compact poetic art-form originating in Japan, describing a momentary experience that could be likened to a 'sacrament of the present moment'. It is 'a way of looking at the physical world and seeing something deeper, like the very nature of existence' (YourDictionary website). A thought or feeling is expressed within a set number of syllables, usually with reference to a season, nature or weather. It doesn't rhyme; its flow lies in its concentrated form. Two examples:

Temple bells die out.
The fragrant blossoms remain.
A perfect evening!
Basho Matsuo, 1644–94

Winter assaults us
Prayer freezes and will not rise –
Seasons come and go.
Janet Lunt

In what season do you see your soul at the moment? What colours might describe that? To express this, try one of the following, in conversation with God:

- With pencil crayons or paint, create a picture to describe the season you find yourself in.
- Have a go at writing a haiku, capturing the present season of the soul, in one verse or more. Although strictly it should consist of 17 syllables set in three short lines (5–7–5, or 6–5–6), hinting at nature, weather or season, exceptions abound (see below).

a mountain of stars –
the never-ending reach
of forgiveness

in the space
between words…
worlds

Authors unknown

Bleak midwinter (1)

Reflective

Although a little early, it seems appropriate to look at a Christmas carol that pursues a wintry theme. Slowly read through the first verse of the famous carol by Christina Rossetti, allowing the sense of frozen paralysis to take hold.

In the bleak midwinter, frosty wind made moan,
Earth stood hard as iron, water like a stone;
Snow had fallen, snow on snow, snow on snow,
In the bleak midwinter, long ago.

Rossetti paints a scene frozen to a standstill, devoid of growth and sustenance. This is her description of the world before Christ's incarnation – of its frozen heart if you like – in need of spring, of God's intervention.

Quite suddenly, Rossetti turns our attention in verse 2 to God, who is vast beyond imagining; yet… he is content with an animal shed! It is so extraordinary that it is almost outrageous. Read the next two verses below, and spend time reflecting in awe on how our Maker came among us in our hard, frozen, helpless state.

Our God, Heaven cannot hold Him, nor earth sustain;
Heaven and earth shall flee away when He comes to reign.
In the bleak midwinter a stable place sufficed
The Lord God Almighty, Jesus Christ.

Enough for Him, whom cherubim worship night and day,
A breastful of milk, and a mangerful of hay;
Enough for Him, whom angels fall down before,
The ox and ass and camel which adore.

Remember and give thanks for the times God has come to you in a helpless state or impasse.

Bleak midwinter (2)

Imaginative/intercession

Angels and archangels may have gathered there,
Cherubim and seraphim thronged the air;
But His mother only, in her maiden bliss,
Worshipped the beloved with a kiss.

Stay in your imagination with the bitter-cold scene of verse 1, but now in pitch darkness, the sort of night when the world would not venture out. Stand beneath the stars, your fingers and toes aching with cold. You see a thin, golden glow seeping from beneath the dog-eared door of an insignificant shed. Something unseen is happening inside. (Rossetti has shared the secret.) The light that leaks from beneath the door is the brightness of heavenly presence, mingled with the glowing warmth of human love and devotion.

Now watch over time as this golden light begins to seep out along the ground... towards the fields... reaching houses in the town... spreading throughout the land... across oceans to all lands... melting hardness and dispelling darkness in its wake. As you envisage this, pray for dark or frozen areas that come to mind in the world or that affect individuals: that the light and wisdom of Christ and the heat of heavenly love will melt or transform them.

Bleak midwinter (3)

Poetry

Having been drawn into the intimacy of the first moments of the incarnation, the last verse of Rossetti's carol enables us to respond in heartfelt worship.

> *What can I give Him, poor as I am?*
> *If I were a shepherd, I would bring a lamb;*
> *If I were a Wise Man, I would do my part;*
> *Yet what I can I give Him: give my heart.*

Worship includes both the offering of our lips and what we do with our lives. Can you think back to that moment when you first felt quickened to respond to God in Jesus? Below is a poem by Charlotte Mew (1869–1928), which uses winter imagery as an aid to a moment of being called.

The Call

From our low seat beside the fire
Where we have dozed and dreamed and watched the glow
Or raked the ashes, stopping so
We scarcely saw the sun or rain
Above or looked much higher
Than this same quiet red and burned-out fire.
Tonight we heard a call,

A rattle on the window pane,
A voice on the sharp air,
And felt a breath stirring our hair.
A flame within us, something swift and tall
Swept in and out and that was all.
Was it a bright or a dark angel? Who can know?
It left no mark upon the snow,
But suddenly it snapped the chain,
Unbarred, flung wide the door
Which will not shut again;
And so we cannot sit here any more
We must arise and go:
The world is cold without
And dark and hedged about
With mystery and enmity and doubt,
But we must go
Though yet we do not know
What marks we shall leave upon the snow.

Reflect on your sense of calling as you look ahead. What marks do you hope to leave in the snow? Talk with God about it.

The saints of Advent

Anne Noble

Cloud of witnesses

Introduction

Throughout the year, the Church of England celebrates men and women of faith, some of whom are known as saints. Even when we know little about them, something of their story can be inspirational as well as challenging on our own faith journeys. There are many commemorations during the season of Advent and, in these reflections, we will concentrate on the stories of four: Nicholas, Lucy, Flannan (one of the Irish Peregrini) and Eglantyne Jebb, who cofounded Save the Children. Each section will feature a short introduction to the saint followed by reflections on the key features of their stories. To explore more of their stories and the modern traditions associated with them, your local library or the internet may be helpful.

Begin by reading Hebrews 12:1–2. Here, the saints of heaven are described as a 'cloud of witnesses' surrounding us as we run the race of life towards Jesus. In my imagination, this crowd is like that at a marathon, the supporters who wait for the runners, especially those who are family and friends. Who in your life has cheered you on your way? Maybe they were part of your life for a long time or maybe they appear briefly, at a moment of significance. Give thanks to God for them. This is also a passage which reminds us that the goal of our life is Jesus Christ. All the people whose stories we are exploring here had their Christian faith at the centre of their lives. Advent can so easily be hurried through in all the preparations for Christmas. Instead, take some time each day throughout the season to focus on the presence of God.

To help you centre on God, you might like to set up a small space in your home as a reminder. Place a candle, an open Bible or a cross in the place where you pray. Write the names of those you have remembered on to card or pieces of paper – you could add a photograph if you have one. Place these as a reminder of the 'cloud of witnesses' that surround you. You might like to add the names of Nicholas, Lucy, Flannan and Eglantyne Jebb as we learn a little more of them. Spend time in this place every day, remembering that God is with you and that God loves you. If it helps, try repeating the words of Psalm 46:10: 'Be still and know that I am God.' Stay here as long as you need or can manage each day.

St Nicholas (6 December)

Spotlight

There is little concrete information about St Nicholas. He was bishop of Myra (Lycia in modern Turkey) in the early fourth century. It is believed that he survived the persecution of Diocletian and died peacefully in old age around AD343. He is the patron saint of children and sailors. Over the years, the figure of St Nicholas became merged with other stories from Nordic folklore to produce our modern Santa Claus. However, modern representations of Santa can seem a long way removed from Nicholas' example of the generous and compassionate Christian life focused on those who were vulnerable and at risk.

One story tells of a dowry given to three girls to prevent them being sold into prostitution. Wishing to remain anonymous, St Nicholas threw the gold through their open window at night, where it fell into their stockings or shoes. Another relates how, when returning by sea from a visit to the Holy Land, a fierce storm blew up. Concerned for the sailors, Nicholas prayed and the storm was calmed.

Pause for a moment to think of both these legends. When have you received the generosity of others? Have you ever been in a frightening situation when someone prayed? What do you remember of those occasions and how they felt? Give thanks to God for that person or people and add their names to the cloud of witnesses you began earlier.

Lord God, thank you for those who have inspired us on our journey of faith. Help us to pass that on and to be an example of your love to others. Amen

Suffer little children

Imaginative

We often hear the phrase, 'Christmas is a time for children'. The Christmas story is, of course, a story for *everyone*: young or old, weak or strong. The Gospel reading for St Nicholas (as patron saint for children) is Mark 10:13–16. This passage recounts the moment when parents brought their children to Jesus. Today we read that story reflectively, finding our place within it. If you struggle with childhood for any reason, you might either want to skip this reflection or make sure you have someone to whom you can speak afterwards.

Read Mark 10:13–16 slowly. Imagine the scene. Jesus has been teaching his disciples inside a house; now families are pressing at the door trying to get in. Maybe the group has moved outside the building. Where do you imagine that you are? Stay with this place. What do you see or hear?

Hear the voices of the disciples. What are they doing and saying? What might you think or feel if you were one of those trying to reach Jesus and someone was preventing the crowd from getting near him? Offer those feelings to God.

Jesus is angry and raises his voice above the others. He bids the children come in and gives them his blessing, laying hands upon them. Can you envisage an angry Jesus? Jesus stands with the weak and the vulnerable in society. Where are those people in your life or at your church? Is that perhaps you?

Now Jesus speaks again, asking us to be childlike in our approach to the kingdom. Pause and reflect on your own life. What do you think are the childlike qualities he sees in you?

Where are you in the story? Remain in the quietness and hold all your reflections and any concerns before God. Remember that, in God's eyes, we are all God's beloved children. Hear God's voice welcoming you into his presence, feel his hands on your head and receive his blessing. Stay in that moment for as long as you are able.

God, you have created us and you welcome us as your children. Help us to simply be who we are in your presence and receive your blessing with wonder and love. Amen

An Advent stocking

Creative

St Nicholas' gifts are said to have fallen into stockings or shoes. Find an old sock. You might wish to decorate it.

Every day during Advent, place in or near the sock something that you can give away next year. Some suggestions might be: gifts of money, gifts to local charities, pledges of time or something personal to you. Your gifts can reflect your situation and what you are able to give.

Generous God, thank you for the example of Nicholas, whose life of generosity and compassion reached out with practical love to the vulnerable. Help us to be generous in our turn and, when we need it, to accept the generosity of others with grace. Amen

St Lucy (13 December)

Creative

The story of Lucy is largely unknown. She was a young woman who was martyred at Syracuse in Sicily during the persecutions of Diocletian in AD303–4. The legend is that she was betrayed as a Christian by the man to whom she was betrothed when she gave away her dowry in gifts to the poor. Whatever the facts for Lucy, it is the case that Christians of that era and since have been betrayed by friends, family and lovers to the authorities and suffered persecution at all levels. Lucy's story reflects real life for many people.

The name Lucy means 'light' in Latin. In Sweden, 13 December is marked by special services and processions in which boys and girls wear crowns of lights. Light through darkness is a key theme for Advent, when we anticipate the coming of Jesus, the light of the world, at Christmas and his return at the end of time.

Read Luke 11:33–36, the Gospel passage set for the celebration of St Lucy. Notice how many times a word for light or a word which indicates light is used. In the next week and beyond, commit to doing one or both of the activities below.

Christmas lights

During Advent, many houses are decorated with lights ready for Christmas. These strings of lights can become a kind of rosary. As you travel, use houses which are lit in this way as a reminder to pray for the light of Christ to shine in your community.

Turning the lights on and off

Every time you turn out a light, say a prayer for those who find darkness difficult or are in dark places themselves. Most of us will know someone. Pray for yourself if that is you.

You might like to use the traditional evening collect:

Lighten our darkness, O Lord, we pray, and by Thy Great Mercy defend us from all perils and dangers of this night, for the love of Thine only son, our Saviour, Jesus Christ. Amen.

A litany of light for Advent

Litany

Pray the following litany as a way of interceding for some of your 'witnesses', or for anyone else who comes to mind.

In creation, the Spirit hovered over chaos and darkness and God's voice spoke light.
For those who struggle in chaotic lives – Let there be light.

God led the people of the exodus through the night by a pillar of fire.
For those who are lost and cannot find their way – Let there be light.

The Lord is my light and my salvation (Psalm 27:1).
For those who need salvation – Let there be light.

God shines his light into the dark places we would hide, and reveals sin of thought and deed.
For those who struggle with sin – Let there be light.

The light shines in the darkness, and the darkness did not overcome it (John 1:5).
For those who are ill or dying – Let there be light.

The people who walked in darkness have seen a great light (Isaiah 9:2). God's light reveals a new future.
For all of us as we take each step forward – Let there be light.

Jesus Christ was raised in the dawning of a new resurrection day.
In all new beginnings – Let there be light.

Ordinary pots

Creative

Read 2 Corinthians 4:6–15, the epistle reading set for St Lucy.

On a trip to Orkney, we visited 'The Tomb of the Eagles'. The name of this Neolithic burial site comes from the many eagle talons buried alongside the human remains. Nearby are the remains of the houses these people may have lived in. We were given the privilege of handling some of the finds associated with their homes. Among these were the remains of a clay bowl. Our guide pointed out small half-moon incisions in its rim. As I held this broken vessel, the guide suggested that the maker had used his or her thumb nail to decorate the unbaked clay. Placing our own thumb nails into the marks that had been left there connected us to a people who had lived 5,000 years before. Their ordinary cooking pot became an extraordinary connection to their lives.

In the passage from 2 Corinthians, Paul writes of how we are like ordinary clay jars which hold the extraordinary treasure of God. We become connected to God in the treasure of his life held within us. Lucy is remembered because of her belief that the presence of Jesus in her life was a treasure worth everything, even her life. Sometimes ordinary people can do extraordinary things.

If you have clay or plasticine, use it to make a small bowl. It doesn't have to be a work of art! Decorate your bowl using something ordinary, perhaps your own finger nails if you are working with clay.

If you can't do this, use a bowl you already have. Place it on a sheet of paper and add your decorations to that. Place a small cross (you could make one from paper) within it. Place the bowl with your 'cloud of witnesses'. Pray for those whose seemingly ordinary lives are, or were, lived by the extraordinary truth of the gospel. Pray that God may use you to shine in the world for his glory.

God of complex, fragile beauty, you entrust to us your light and we find our life in you. Hold us amidst life's pressures and help us when we feel weak. Amen

St Flannan: pilgrim and missionary (18 December)

Creative

Flannan is celebrated by the Irish church on 18 December, marking his death in AD640. His oratory sits next to Killaloe Cathedral in County Clare, Ireland. Flannan is known as one of the Peregrini who travelled over water and land spreading the good news of Jesus. Sometimes these pilgrims were known as the 'people of the coracle', a reference to the small, circular craft which they used to cross water. Coracles can be strapped to the shoulders when the traveller takes to the land. If Flannan used such a vessel, we might imagine him afloat and walking, carrying his coracle with him as both shelter and transport. We can also imagine what it would be like to steer such a light craft through the water: idyllic and peaceful in good weather; simply clinging on in swifter moving and more turbulent currents. It is a powerful image of how life's journey can seem: peaceful or even becalmed at times, followed by periods when we feel like we are simply hanging on.

Find a reasonably large bowl and fill it with water. Find or make something that will float to be a 'coracle': half a walnut shell, a small shell or anything else you might have. You could simply float a small piece of paper on the water.

Let the water be still – think of the still places and quiet waters in your life's journey at the moment. Offer those places to God.

Stir the water gently. Imagine yourself in the coracle. How does it feel to be carried by the water? Do you ever experience God carrying you in this way?

Agitate the water. As the craft is tossed about, think of places in your life which feel disturbed. Now let the water return to stillness and watch what happens. Ask God to bring you his peace. Stay in this moment for as long as you are able.

Three Advent peregrinations

Going out/creative

A peregrination is the journey undertaken by a pilgrim such as Flannan. Advent invites us to a slower pace, like Flannan who walked his pilgrimages.

Here are three suggestions for peregrinations to slow down your Advent journey in the frenzied rush towards Christmas. You could try all three or select the one which best suits you.

1 The peregrination of our work and/or neighbourhood

Set aside some time to explore your place of work and/or the neighbourhood in which you live. You may have some idea where you will go, or not; the idea is to 'wander' and it doesn't matter whether you go a long way or just a few metres. When something catches your attention, try to stay with it for as long as you feel comfortable. What do you notice, what attracts you, what repels you, what prayer forms in your heart? What do you notice differently because you have slowed down? Give these things to God.

2 The peregrination of our homes

Taking the same approach, move through your home. Where do you feel drawn? What do you notice there? Does this space speak of God? What prayer forms in your heart? Give this to God.

3 The peregrination of our hearts and minds

Settle in a space where you feel comfortable. This might be a quiet place or, if you are an extrovert, somewhere livelier. What are you seeking or hoping for in life? As you look forward to next year, where do you hope the journey might lead? What have been the surprises of this last year? Where has God led you that you didn't expect to go? What has changed in your journey with God?

Draw or write a map of your peregrinations. Where has the Spirit taken your wanderings? Has any pattern emerged?

> *Creator God, help us to notice the things that stay the same and those things that change. Help us to explore your world and notice where you are at work.*
>
> *Christ our light, you guided Flannan and led him to places and people to share your gospel. Give us courage to follow you with senses set to notice the people we encounter on our way.*
>
> *Holy Spirit, you inspire and enable our journey. In the familiar, help us to find your presence. May we know your guidance in our futures. Amen*

Eglantyne Jebb (17 December)

Spotlight/intercession

Eglantyne Jebb was born in Shropshire in 1876. She studied at Oxford, developing an interest in social concerns, and became a teacher, though when her health broke down she left to live with her mother in Cambridge.

Pause: Recall times when your plans and dreams were changed by circumstance or ill health. Ask God to show or remind you how he was present in those times.

In 1912, Eglantyne travelled to Macedonia to work with refugees there. During that time (World War I and afterwards), she saw first-hand the effect of allied blockades on civilian populations. She was particularly horrified by what was happening to children. In 1919, together with her sister Dorothy Buxton, she campaigned to end the blockade and establish a League of Nations. She was arrested during a rally in Trafalgar Square and fined. The story goes that she impressed the court so much that the prosecuting council gave her the money for the fine.

Pause: It is difficult to speak truth to power. Pray for all those who, despite being in weak and vulnerable places in society, are prepared to speak up, especially whistle-blowers, human-rights campaigners and those who defend the vulnerable against injustice. You might pray too for the court officials, lawyers, barristers, solicitors and judges who deal with such cases.

In May 1919, Eglantyne and Dorothy hired the biggest venue they could find, the Albert Hall, in order to promote their campaign. It was the moment Save the Children was launched. Instead of anticipated opposition, the sisters found support and the money raised went straight towards aid for the children whose plight they highlighted. In 1923, Eglantyne wrote the 'Declaration of the Rights of the Child'. The current United Nations Convention of the Rights of Children is derived from her work.

Pause: Pray for children in this country and throughout the world who are at risk. You might like to pray particularly for those charities and non-governmental organisations which seek to bring them aid. If it helps and you are able, you could look on their individual websites for specific areas to pray about.

Nothing is impossible for God

Creative

> Save the Children is sometimes told that reaching its aims is impossible. But, as our founder Eglantyne Jebb said, it is only impossible if we refuse to attempt it.
>
> HRH The Princess Royal, President (Save the Children)

Eglantyne Jebb spoke up on behalf of people who had no voice at a time when her own voice, as a woman, would struggle to be heard. In so doing, she brought hope into a seemingly hopeless situation. We can only wonder at how many lives may have been saved by her courage and conviction. Such hope is defiant, refusing to believe that nothing can be done, believing instead that another world is possible.

Read Isaiah 61:1–4 and 8–11, one of the passages set for the Sundays in Advent. Here, the prophet speaks to the Jews who have been in exile in Babylon as they return to Jerusalem. Many of them have died; families have been torn apart; their beloved city has been devastated; the temple, the house of God, has been sacked. Yet, inspired by God, Isaiah affirms hope in God – this is trust, belief, desire and determination; it is faith in God's promise that God intends a new beginning for the people of God. His words ask the people to imagine the future God has for them and so begin to make it real. Prophets both speak to situations as they are and speak of God's vision for the people.

Read verse 11 again. The verse speaks of the hope of a garden sown in spring coming to life later in the year. All seeds are sown with this hope. Find a seed, perhaps saving the pips from an orange or apple. In a quiet space, hold the seed in your hand. Wonder at the potential it holds, all that it can become. Reflect on what the seed will need to grow. Imagine it growing. What will develop from your seed? Give thanks for all those, like Eglantyne Jebb, who plant seeds of hope in the world.

You could write out the words of Isaiah 61:11 on a card and place your seed with it. Place the seed in the space you created at the beginning of these sessions. Let it be a reminder to you of God's possibilities in the world.

Agents of hope

Reflective

Something about the saints, including those within our own cloud of witnesses, brings hope that we can make a difference in the world. Such differences can be on the smaller scale of ordinary living, a kindness shared or a word of hope spoken.

Hope is one of Advent's great themes: the hope of the coming of Jesus into the world, both as the baby of Bethlehem and as a returning king. Such hope has inspired humanity through the ages to build a better world and change lives for the better.

Return to your cloud of witnesses. Find somewhere comfortable to sit and lay their names out around you. Imagine them all, and yourself in Jesus' presence. On this final day of reflection, spend some time concentrating on yourself. What do you hope for as this year draws to a close? What hope do you need at this moment? How are you an agent of hope to those you know?

Repeat Psalm 62:5 to yourself: 'For God alone my soul waits in silence, for my hope is from him.' Spend as much time as you need with this verse. Listen with your heart for God to speak his hope to you.

Advent: anticipation and preparation

Liz Hoare

Why Advent?

Introduction

Are you the kind of person who goes overboard preparing for Christmas, or do you put it off till the last minute, rushing out on Christmas Eve to buy last-minute gifts? Would you like the approach to Christmas to be different this year? For a consumerist society, I expect it will be as frantic and materialistic as ever, but God's kingdom has always challenged the prevailing outlook, inviting us to dance to a different tune. Advent expresses and summarises the gospel in its totality. It is the beginning of the church's year, but it confronts us with momentous things: heaven and hell, death and judgement, known as the Four Last Things. No wonder we only get ready for Christmas – a birth is so much safer than such cataclysmic events. How could we anticipate and prepare for them?

Advent exists to help us prepare for a kingdom which has yet to find its complete fulfilment and will only do so when Christ comes again in glory. This is where the real focus of Advent lies. It is full of mystery and majesty, the big themes of life. Its song is about expectancy, watchfulness, deep, deep longing and a call to wake up and be ready. It's a challenge to the prevailing noise, to complacency and to our human tendency to grow deaf. Its themes are a long way from chocolate Advent calendars and all the superficial razzmatazz of the run-up to Christmas, which is how we often experience this season.

The theme of anticipation and preparation for this Advent season in *Quiet Spaces* offers an invitation to set some time aside to press 'pause' and meet, in our own day-to-day experience, the God who has come and who will come again. We may do so because in between those two climactic events, God calls to us in a myriad of ways that are designed to draw us closer to himself and know him in the present.

We are fortunate in the Western hemisphere in that the seasons assist our imaginations as the year turns. The old year is dying and the days are short. It's dark outside. We are watching and waiting for the light to come with the life it brings.

What thoughts come to mind when you hear the word 'anticipation'? Are they positive and hopeful or negative and fearful? What do you anticipate with longing? And what fills you with dread?

Talk to God about your reactions.

Spotlight on time

Creative

One of the problems with anticipation around Christmas is the fact we have been here before and know what happened. It all feels so familiar and, anyway, how can we create excitement about something that has already happened? God did become flesh and blood in Jesus, but we are called to live in the light of that now.

This is precisely where Advent can help us, because of the way it deals with time. Time past and time future are both essential as we approach the second as well as the first coming of God to his world, but there is also time present, for discipleship is lived in the here and now. Most of us are rarely fully present; our minds are focusing on something from the past or looking ahead to what is coming next. Advent invites us to live more fully in the present as we wait in anticipation for its climax. When we were children, my brother and I used to vie with one another to be first to open the Advent calendar window and tick off another day in the approach to Christmas. Rather than ticking off the days, Advent is about living fully in the now and expecting to find God there.

This Advent, as you make preparations for Christmas, try to keep your full attention on what you are doing in the present and turn whatever it is into prayer. We can pray in the midst of ordinary tasks like wrapping presents and we can also turn that task into prayer. Wrapping a present, for example, might nudge us to pray for the person receiving it or give thanks for the gifts of God in Jesus. You could then take this way of praying with the ordinary further and reflect on yourself as a giver of gifts and what you would like God to help you to grow in your character. What gifts could you bring to others with the help of God's grace?

Many people are trapped by something in the past that keeps dragging them back, or they are anxious about the future. Knowing that God is Lord of all time and that he sees it all from beginning to end, yet still meets us in the present moment, is a liberating gift that Advent offers, for it invites us to look back into history when God was at work and also to look forward to the end of time when he will fully establish his rule upon earth. Advent calendars are not just for children, for as we deliberately pause to mark time, we may also be more aware and able to recognise God's presence with us in that moment.

Preparing in Advent

Creative

The Jesse tree, a decorative journey through the story of the Bible, has introduced many to the idea of Jesus' ancestors and God's long-planned promise of deliverance through the line of David.

Some churches and cathedrals depict the Jesse tree in stained glass or paint; you might like to research whether there is one near you and go to see it. Similarly, an Advent wreath has four candles, one for each of the Sundays in Advent, representing those who anticipated the coming of God to his people: the patriarchs, the prophets, John the Baptist and Mary, the mother of Jesus.

You might also make your own Jesse tree or Advent wreath. Instructions for both of these can easily be found online, and often include Bible passages that tell us more about the characters involved. These are both creative tasks that focus on biblical characters whose lives give us food for thought. They remind us that God's great acts in history involve all kinds of people – from kings to peasant girls – and the Jesse tree especially encourages us to see ourselves as part of God's great family tree, for in Christ we are his children. If you prefer a ready-made daily visual reminder of the way Advent helps us prepare for Christ's coming, an Advent calendar that has a biblical theme rather than chocolate is a good way to ensure that each day includes a chance to pause and recollect God's presence in the now.

Stock of Jesse

Going out

Read Isaiah 11:1–4a.

Both Matthew's and Luke's Gospels include genealogies for Jesus. Matthew's tracing of Jesus' ancestry back to Abraham through David also includes Jesse. In the Isaiah passage, the prophet foretells a shoot coming from the stock of Jesse (v. 1). It is a vivid image. A gnarled tree stump, covered with moss and lichen: could life break out from such an unpromising source? But God says it will and, what is more, this life will come from his Spirit and exhibit God-like qualities: wisdom and understanding, counsel and might, knowledge, fear of the Lord and righteousness.

Tracing the coming of Christ into the world back into the history of God's people like this shows that God was making preparations too. The prophets looked forward with anticipation to the day of the Lord when he would come and establish his rule on earth. The exiled people of Israel in Isaiah's day must have wondered how that could come about, but this prophecy told them to look for life in unexpected places.

If there is a wood nearby, go for a walk there or find a path that includes some trees along the way.

As you walk, reflect on one or more of the qualities that the shoot from the stump of Jesse will display. If you see a tree stump as you walk, pause and look closely. What do you see? Are there any signs of life showing or do you need a lot of imagination to see new life? If you are on a footpath, look out for submerged roots indicating life beneath the surface. Are there unpromising parts of your life at present where you have ceased to anticipate new life? Talk to God about them as you walk, asking for what you need.

Anticipating God's promises

Spotlight

There are four Sundays in Advent and, traditionally, each week is designated to particular biblical characters: patriarchs, prophets, John the Baptist and Mary. As we have seen, Advent wreaths represent these, with a candle to be lit each successive week in the season.

Abraham and Sarah are examples of two people who were given a promise that required them to wait a long time before they experienced its fulfilment.

The prophets spoke to the whole nation, descended from Abraham and Sarah, with words of hope and of judgement. Their hearers must have dreaded the approach of God's judgement, even as they clung to his promise of forgiveness and restoration.

John the Baptist was the last of the prophets, and stood in the gap between the old and the new age. His message filled his followers with anticipation as he called them to 'Prepare the way of the Lord'. He lived to see the Messiah of whom he prophesied.

Mary's 'Yes' to God meant that her whole life became caught up in the final preparation for the birth of the Saviour and the subsequent unfolding of the life, death and resurrection of her son.

None of these characters could foresee the details of what they anticipated and waited for; they could only wait in trust and dependence on God's word and his faithful character.

The great banquet

Bible reading

Read Luke 14:15–24.

When did you last look forward to a meal? You may have been doing manual work for some hours and gained a healthy appetite. You may have looked forward to a special meal with friends or family to celebrate an occasion like a birthday. Perhaps there was a day when you felt ready for a tasty meal after a bout of illness that had dulled your appetite.

In Jesus' parable of the great banquet, as told by Luke, the guests invited to the dinner were not looking forward to it at all, because they were distracted by other things. One by one, they gave their excuses and so missed out on a momentous event. Banquets in the Gospel are a key feature of the kingdom of God, so these people were rejecting God's invitation to be part of something with eternal consequences. In their place, the crippled, blind and lame were brought in, and then some more from the highways and byways until the places were filled. None of the guests had done anything at all to deserve their place: no preparation, no anticipation, yet suddenly there they were, propelled right into the kingdom.

Preparation can sometimes mean doing less rather than more.

When is it time to stop making preparations and let go? Waiting, listening and watching are part of Advent preparations too.

We know that some preparations are required in life, a special meal being a good example. Some preparations involve stilling our minds and bodies so that we are open and receptive. Watching animals and birds in their natural habitat is a good example. We await with breathless anticipation, aware of the need to be fully present to whatever is to come.

Is there something on your to-do list that you could let go of in order to make room for whatever God wants to provide?

Maranatha: 'Come, Lord Jesus'

Intercession

The way we pray during Advent will be determined by whether we see the coming of Christ as a promise or a threat. Our response will affect our decisions, our lifestyle choices, our planning for the future and the way we view the world and everyone in it. For Christians, Advent is full of hope as well as longing, and these two features can shape our desires and our prayers.

The early Christians lived with acute anticipation of God's coming, which shaped their identity in the world. They had a prayer that was also a watchword: '*Maranatha*': 'Come, Lord Jesus.' It is the final prayer in the Bible in Revelation 22:20. These Christians longed for God to come and vindicate them in a way that persecuted Christians today might be best placed to understand. This verse follows a promise by Jesus himself saying, 'Surely I am coming soon.'

Jesus refers to himself as the bright morning star, something that sentinels on night watch look out for, as it heralds the dawn and the coming of the light. Everything in creation that loves the Lord stands on tiptoe with yearning: everyone who hears, everyone who is thirsty, everyone in need of the water of life (Revelation 22:17).

Today, try listening to the news on the radio or select some news items online, and pray for each situation with the watchword '*Maranatha*' in mind.

Watching with anticipation

Meditative

Waiting is not necessarily a passive, empty experience. We can wait with anticipation, as we have already seen in connection with watching wildlife. In the Bible, waiting is closely associated with watching, and watching is a frame of mind, an attitude. We have to practise.

Waiting and watching with anticipation in Advent can be a rich and strangely fulfilling activity. It offers time to pause and step aside from the mad run-up to Christmas, and allows the mystery of the coming of God into the world to captivate our hearts and imaginations afresh. But we have to find ways to practise what is in fact a spiritual discipline. It is very countercultural to wait and allow the sense of anticipation to do its work. It is one of the reasons why Christmas Day can seem such an anticlimax when it arrives; we have already eaten the mince pies, sung our favourite carols and overloaded our homes with yet more consumer goods. The only way to escape the lure of the now is to listen to our deeper desires for love and fulfilment and to seek the source of lasting satisfaction.

Close to the end of his first letter to the Corinthians, the apostle Paul gave some final instructions for people who are waiting with longing and expectation for the coming of the Lord Jesus: 'Keep alert, stand firm in your faith, be courageous, be strong. Let all that you do be done in love' (1 Corinthians 16:13–14). He could say this because his readers knew that God had come in Jesus; they had met him in their hearts and looked forward to seeing him face to face. One simple way of practising waiting intentionally is to sit by a window where you can see a bird table and watch the activity there. As with the exercise of wrapping presents, practise turning what you see into prayer.

O come, Emmanuel

Poetry

For centuries, the church has used a number of prayers called antiphons during Advent, placed before and after the saying of the Magnificat. They are known as the great 'O's because each one begins 'O', followed by an image representing a title for the coming Messiah. There are seven of them: O Wisdom, O Lord, O Root of Jesse, O Key of David, O Morning Star, O King of the Nations, O Emmanuel. The antiphons all call on Christ to come and express the depths of yearning that we feel for a world needing to be saved and transformed.

The great 'O's draw attention to some of the ways human beings have tried to understand and speak of God. They also offer a marked contrast to the contemporary world. Thus 'O Wisdom' rather than data; 'O Lord' rather than power-crazed, earth-bound rulers; 'O Root of Jesse', stretching deep and far back rather than the superficial offering of immediacy and disconnect; 'O Key of David', challenging how we perceive and receive Jesus; 'O Morning Star', bringing hope rather than despair and empty promises of improved standards of living; 'O King of the Nations', inviting us to catch a bigger vision than our small-minded parochial horizons;

and 'O Emmanuel', the God who is with us, seeking to draw our attention from our trivial pursuits and personal preoccupations to rest and see and put our faith in his faithfulness to us.

Many people find poetry helpful as a way in to prayer and expressing what God means to them. There are a number of anthologies designed to be used in Advent. One by Malcolm Guite called *Waiting on the Word* (Canterbury Press, 2015) contains a number by the author himself based on the Great 'O's and each one has a short reflection on the imagery. If you can get hold of this book, read through a few. Or you could search online for other poems based on the antiphons.

As you turn these mysterious 'O' names over in your mind, settle on one as an image for your own longings and needs this Advent time.

Darkness to light

Reflective

One of my favourite moments in Advent in recent years was at an Advent carol service as the congregation waited in darkness for the service to begin. In the inky black stillness, there was a sense of breathless anticipation and, suddenly, a crystal-clear voice rang out: 'I look from afar: and lo, I see the power of God coming, and a cloud covering the whole earth. Go ye out to meet him and say: Art thou he that should come to rule?' Slowly, candles were lit around the church and the readings and carols got under way.

There was something very powerful about the gradual transformation of the darkness, which spoke of the light of Christ shining in the darkness of the world. Isaiah 9:2 says, 'The people who walked in darkness have seen a great light; those who lived in a land of deep darkness – on them light has shined.' Did you know that a lighted match can be seen a mile away in thick darkness?

Take some time to reflect on the impact of light in the darkness today, preferably at night when artificial light of some kind is needed. If you can sit in the darkness for a while and then light a candle or switch on a torch, you may find this an aid to your imagination. What is it like to imagine yourself as a light in the darkness? Jesus said, 'I am the light of the world. Whoever follows me will never walk in darkness' (John 8:12), but he also said that we are lights of the world too (Matthew 5:14). We cannot ignite this light within ourselves; it is a gift of God who dwells in us by his Spirit.

End this time by thanking God for his gift of light, and pray for those who are seeking to be lights in dark places of the world. If you lit a candle for this time, it may act as a reminder of the power of the light of Christ.

Mary's song

Creative

Read Luke 1:39–56.

Few things lead to anticipation and preparation like pregnancy. How would Mary have prepared for this strange birth that she had not sought but had assented to? Surely there was apprehension as well as anticipation in her young heart? In our Western material world, preparation looks very visible as we buy endless pieces of kit that we think we will need for a new baby, but the real preparation takes place in the darkness of the womb. The mother-to-be can provide conditions that help, through rest and healthy habits, but mostly she simply waits until the time is right.

As a pregnant mother-to-be, Mary would have discovered the importance of waiting for her baby to come to full term and be born. She had plenty of time to ponder the angel's message to her and wonder what God was up to. Her visit to her cousin

Elizabeth and her joy expressed in her exuberant song which we call the Magnificat suggests that she had thought deeply about the meaning of God's word to her. Her anticipation is not just about her own story, but about God's wider purposes for his people Israel and beyond. Her song presents an upside-down world where the mighty are brought low and the lowly exalted (v. 52) but her main focus is on God himself, her Saviour, the Mighty One (vv. 47, 49).

Mary's relationship with her cousin and her joyful song show that she had used the waiting time wisely by focusing on the inner preparation of the heart. Mary's song draws on the Old Testament (see, for example, the story of Hannah in 1 Samuel 1—2) to show how the God of Israel, who acted in history to save his people, is acting to do so again.

How do we put into words what our relationship with God is like? Reflecting on Mary, might you take a pen and write a song of praise to God as part of your heart's preparation for the coming of the Saviour?

Anticipating the kingdom

Reflective

Read Isaiah 35.

Isaiah presents us with a wonderful picture of healing and wholeness in his visual image of a world restored. Everything is as it should be in this glorious picture of restoration. Picture the desert bursting into life, flowers and lush grass replacing the parched bare earth. There are wonderful promises for creation here but also for human beings, especially the fearful, frail and needy. The blind will see and the lame 'leap like a deer' (v. 6). If this sounds familiar, it is because Jesus himself took these words and made them his own, enacting them in his ministry on earth (Matthew 11:4–5). Hundreds of years separated Isaiah and Jesus, but the prophet was not only looking forward to his people going home, he was also, whether he knew it or not, speaking of the Incarnation.

The people who received Isaiah's vision were still in exile and home was a long way off. They were still coming to terms with what had happened and the future did not look hopeful. Could they imagine walking on that highway, the Holy Way (v. 8), ransomed and redeemed? Would their voices ever lift again in songs of joy, sorrow and sighing having fled away (v. 10)? There are many reasons to despair today as we look around at the world, and maybe situations close to us give us cause for sorrow and hopelessness. Isaiah's words still hold true: 'Here is your God... he will come and save you' (v. 4). This is the message of the first Christmas and the one we are preparing for now; in the future, it will be fully realised in a world transformed. This is something not only to anticipate and yearn for in our hearts, but to pray and join in working for as people of the light.

See amid the winter's snow

Andrea Skevington

See amid the winter's snow

Introduction/reflective

See, amid the winter's snow,
Born for us on Earth below,
See, the tender Lamb appears,
Promised from eternal years.

Hail, thou ever blessed morn,
Hail redemption's happy dawn,
Sing through all Jerusalem,
Christ is born in Bethlehem.

Looking through the eyes of the author of this hymn, Edward Caswall, we are called from the very first word 'see'. This hymn, published in 1858 and preserved in hymn books and carol collections, offers us fresh eyes – eyes to see that there is tenderness, love and hope even in the midst of the cold and dark of winter. Above all, we see that Christ stooped down and entered this cold, dark world, laying aside glory and exchanging it for the poverty and straw of a stable. This is grace, that God freely gives, and gives away.

By the time we reach Christmas Eve, many of us are already exhausted by the season, which gives us so much to do. By now, the tinsel may look a little tawdry, and our sense of peace on earth be fraying. This quiet, gentle lyric invites us to pause, to breathe and to see a deep reality behind all this surface.

Over the coming festive days, try to snatch a few moments away from preparations, family and guests; sit quietly and dwell on the words of each verse. Read each line slowly, and let the words unfold before you. If you can, listen to a recording, and hold the carol in your mind as you continue your activities.

See, amid the winter's snow

- What does it mean to open my eyes and see God where I am?
- What does it mean to also acknowledge the coldness and darkness?
- Consider the symbolic power of Christmas at midwinter.

Born for us on Earth below

- Notice the words 'for us' – how wide can you imagine that going?
- How might acknowledging this alter the way we relate to our neighbours near and far?
- Read John 3:16: 'For God so loved the world'. Here, the word 'world' means 'cosmos' in the Greek. What does that mean for you?

See, the tender Lamb appears

- The writer doesn't use the name 'Jesus' or the title 'Christ' in this poem, but a series of images. Why might that be?
- What do you think of this image of the lamb?
- What about 'tender'?
- Consider what it might mean to be tender-hearted today.

Promised from eternal years

- The writer affirms the coming of Jesus has been promised from eternal years – it was always the promise, always the intent. Mull this perspective over in your mind. Is that how you see it?

- Meditate on some of the prophecies we turn to during Advent, for example Isaiah 9:2–7.

As you go to sleep, sing the chorus to yourself, and seek to wake up and greet Christmas morning with those words.

On Christmas Eve, I go outside and gather greenery to decorate the house, winding ivy, putting sprigs of holly about the place. It is a powerful reminder that life will triumph, even in the dead of winter.

If you can, go outside, with friends or family members if you like, and gather greenery. Hold this first verse in your mind. What do you see? Notice the coldness and deadness, but also notice any signs of life and hope. Notice the beauty of all of it. Then, beautify your house with green. As you do so, thank God for Jesus coming into the midst of everyday life, even to your home.

As you handle green living things, remember the prophecy of Isaiah 11:1–9 about a shoot springing up from the old root of Jesse. If you have time, meditate on the passage.

If you cannot go outside, look out of the window, or at pictures of natural beauty.

If you have to work, or run errands, you might like to give something – a green shoot, a warm drink, a mince pie, a Christmas card – to someone you encounter.

Christmas Day

Reflective

Lo, within a manger lies
He who built the starry skies;
He who, throned in height sublime,
Sits among the cherubim.

What does Christmas Day bring for you? Will there be cooking, family, excitement? Will there be work, and celebration? Will there be sadness, an acknowledgement of loss? Will there be loneliness, with or without company, reunions?

Take a few deep calming breaths, and thank God for the promise to be with us in it all.

Let the words of this verse fill your mind. Notice the humility of a manger – the dirt, poverty, cold, exclusion. Think, too, that it is for feeding animals. The lamb lies in a manger. Notice the thread of the imagery.

Then, notice who this is – he who built the starry skies, throned in height sublime. You might like to read John 1:1–5 or Philippians 2:5–11.

Give thanks for this great descent. Know that whatever happens on Christmas Day, joy or sorrow, Jesus is there in the heart of it.

How might knowing that help you? How might it affect your service, conversation, work, celebrating, singing, weeping?

Boxing Day

Action

Say, ye holy shepherds, say,
What your joyful news today;
Wherefore have ye left your sheep
On the lonely mountain steep?

The immediacy of the hymn continues – present tense, speaking directly to the shepherds. As we have been asked to 'see', so they are required to 'say'.

You might like to let the lines run through your mind, and dwell on them as you rest, or tidy, or celebrate.

Say, ye holy shepherds, say

- Think about this exchange – how we ask the shepherds questions, wanting to know what they have to say.
- Think of how, over the Christmas time, you converse with others of different experience. Can we be more open to asking questions, and really attend to the answers? Can we learn from each other?
- Think about the phrase 'holy shepherds'. Can we look for God in unexpected people? Can we learn from those very different from ourselves?
- The joy of the shepherds draws out these questions. What is bringing you joy?

Boxing Day is the traditional day for giving. As we think of the shepherds on their lonely hillside, do you have anything you can give away? You could set aside something from Christmas for those with less.

Dead of night

Going out/creative

As we watched at dead of night,
Lo, we saw a wondrous light:
Angels singing 'Peace On Earth'
Told us of the Saviour's birth.

We have the response to the question in the previous verse, 'Wherefore have you left your sheep on the lonely mountain steep?' We see that it is indeed news they have heard, that peace on earth and the coming of the saviour are announced.

All this happens on a lonely hillside, in the dead of night, to an unlikely group of people.

What does this good news of peace on earth look like to you today? What might it mean to live out of this peaceful news, out of this salvation story, in our dealings with people and the rest of the world today?

> Let us pursue all that makes for peace, and builds up our common life.
>
> Church of England Common Worship, p. 290

Take this quote as your inspiration today.

When it is dark, spend some time outside, or looking out of a window in a dark room. Think about this good news, this brightness, coming at dead of night. The dead of night at the deadest time of midwinter.

What does the dark allow you to see?

Notice any points of brightness. Notice light and sound.

Enter imaginatively into the shepherds' experience.

You might like to write, draw or photograph your own dead of night that you see before you. Pray for light in the darkness and for hope to reach those who feel beyond the reach of hope.

Such a world as this

Creative

Sacred Infant, all divine,
What a tender love was Thine,
Thus to come from highest bliss
Down to such a world as this.

Here we have the heart of the mystery – of incarnation, that God took on flesh; that Jesus emptied himself of bliss, of power, of glory, to come down, down to such a world as this for tender love.

Notice once again the immediacy of the writing, drawing us in. These last two verses are prayers, addressed to Jesus, the sacred infant. Perhaps our practice of looking, of listening, of inviting others to speak, has prepared us for the immediacy of drawing close to Jesus even in the midst of the dead of winter.

Here are two responses to this revelation.

Prayer of thanksgiving

Hold in mind the motive of tender love as you turn to Philippians 2:5–11. Turn this early hymn of praise into a prayer, addressing Jesus directly;

'You did not consider equality with God…' etc.

You might like to write it out in this form, and illustrate or colour around the words, as a meditative prayer.

Practising the presence

What difference does it make to know, if not always to feel, that it was precisely into the darkest and least promising of places and times that Jesus was born? When you reflect on your own dark times, and those of others, can you see means by which the love of God sustained you, and was present with you?

As you pray for others and yourself, hold on to the knowledge that they and you are accompanied in the dark. Pray for an awareness of that presence for those who do not feel it, and ask, with whom can I walk through 'such a world as this'?

To resemble Jesus

Creative

Teach, O teach us, Holy Child,
By Thy face so meek and mild,
Teach us to resemble Thee,
In Thy sweet humility.

So the prayer continues, direct, imperative as ever. We need to learn this – how to resemble Jesus. My friends and I have a saying – 'What does being Jesus-y look like in this situation?' – perhaps a variant on WWJD (What Would Jesus Do?).

We can look into the face of the Holy Child, and ask to be open enough to be transformed into a resemblance. Not that we all become the same, but that we do become the same in this – in our sweetness, our humility and tender love.

Turn to Philippians 2:1–5. See how we are to be imitators of Jesus in this, the laying aside of power, privilege and rightness; learning to think well of others, forbearing from judgement, recognising that we do not have the whole story, knowing that others may have wisdom and insights we lack, knowing that each person is made in the image of God.

> Trample not on any. There may be some work of grace there, that thou knowest not of. The name of God may be written upon that soul thou treadest on, it may be a soul that Christ thought so much of as to give his precious blood for it; therefore, despise it not.
>
> Samuel Taylor Coleridge, quoted by Madeleine L'Engle, *Walking on Water*, p. 125

At Christmas, many of us work hard for others, giving them feasting and fun and presents. By now, we may be exhausted. We may need to care for ourselves. This talk of self-emptying may seem moot, as we are already empty. We must care for ourselves. Jesus did; he took time away and spent nights resting in the Father's love. He spent time with dear friends, he feasted and drank. If you feel empty, remember that you are following the season, and give yourself permission to recharge.

Look around your house or online at pictures of the Christ-child, symbols and representations and words that speak of this self-emptying, this incarnation, this beautiful face.

In prayer, ask to be open to learn.

Draw, write or collage your own representation of this great mystery. What has struck you particularly this Christmas?

This day, or in the days ahead, think about how you can encounter others with humility and grace. Consider experiments in reverse social mobility, in radical generosity, in laying aside status. As we approach the New Year, we can consider how to take the lessons of this Christmas season forward, into the days ahead.

As a Child

Phil Steer

Hinder

> *Let the little children come to me, and do not hinder them, for the kingdom of heaven belongs to such as these.*
>
> MATTHEW 19:14, NIV

The scene for this exchange was, according to Mark's account, a house in Capernaum. Jesus had been with his disciples in Judea, on the other side of the Jordan river, healing and teaching the large crowds that flocked to see him. It had doubtless been a long and tiring day, and now his disciples just wanted a bit of peace and quiet and rest and relaxation after the day's exertions. They also wanted to quiz Jesus about the answer that he'd given to some Pharisees who'd come to test him with a question about divorce. All told, they doubtless just wanted to be left alone and have a little time to themselves. Instead of which, there's a seemingly never-ending stream of people coming to the house, bringing their babies and little children to be touched and prayed for by Jesus. Perhaps the disciples didn't mind too much at first, but after a while they begin to get more and more agitated and irritated, and just want the people and their children to go away and leave them in peace.

It's possible that had the interruption come from someone more 'important', they might not have minded so much. If it had been a religious leader or a Roman centurion or a royal official or a rich young man, it might have been a different matter. Or even if it had been just an 'ordinary' person, but coming for healing from some serious affliction – blindness or leprosy or paralysis, say – again, perhaps the disciples might (albeit grudgingly) have allowed their time with Jesus to be disrupted. But babies and little children! Why, they're too young to understand anything about Jesus; they can't appreciate anything of who he is and what he's come to do. Surely Jesus' time would be better spent teaching those who could understand, accept and follow his teaching, and healing those who could then go and tell others of the healing that they've received? These babies and children couldn't do any of that. And as for the noise and disruption! Babies crying; little children screaming and shouting and running and laughing; their parents and carers admonishing those who have got too excited by it all, and calling after those who have disappeared off into the crowd. Oh no, this is the last thing that Jesus needs! And, truth be told, it is the last thing that the disciples need.

And so the disciples take it upon themselves to act like the entourage of a modern-day celebrity, controlling access to Jesus, allowing through only those whom they deem significant enough to see him, and keeping the rest of the people at bay. And Jesus' response to this? Was he grateful for their intervention and pleased that they had tried to protect his peace and quiet and their chance of some 'quality time' together? Not a bit of it! Mark tells us that Jesus was 'indignant'. He was outraged that his disciples should attempt to keep the little children from seeing him, and just as they had rebuked those who had brought the children, so now Jesus rebuked his disciples.

His anger is hardly surprising when one considers that this all took place not long after the disciples had asked Jesus who was the greatest in the kingdom of heaven, only for him to answer by calling forth a little child. Clearly his disciples had forgotten this already; or perhaps they'd never really understood it in the first place. Perhaps they'd thought that Jesus had been speaking figuratively: that his words applied to those who in some way became like little children, not to the little children themselves. But Jesus' reaction makes clear that this was in no way what he meant. He had called a child to himself not simply as an illustration of what it means to be great in the kingdom of heaven, but because he really wanted the children to come to him.

It is important that we too do not miss the plain meaning of Jesus' message in the rush to apply it to ourselves. Jesus greatly valued the presence of little children, and was eager to spend his time and energy on them, even though they might be too young to understand his teaching, respond to his message and become his disciples. He wasn't looking for any response from them, except perhaps their unselfconscious, heartfelt response to him and to his acceptance and his love.

Sadly, our treatment of children within the church can be rather more like that of the disciples than of Jesus. We don't like the noise and disruption, so we try to keep them quiet and controlled within church, and then parcel them off into their various groups as soon as decently possible, out of sight and out of mind.

I realise, of course, that many churches are far more child-friendly than the picture I've just painted. The church that I've attended for many years has no problem with children wandering around and making a bit of noise during the service and, as I've mentioned, they are actively encouraged to participate enthusiastically during their time of praise and worship. I realise also that there is nothing inherently wrong with children leaving the service to go to their own groups. Nonetheless, I can't help but feel that, even in child-friendly churches, there is still a danger that we might not truly welcome children as Jesus did.

But turning to ourselves, what is it that might hinder the 'little child' in each of us coming to Jesus? My guess is that it will be the very same things that caused the disciples to hinder the little children all those years ago – and which, if we're honest, can cause us to hinder little children today. We're comfortable with our 'adult' approach to Jesus – often so choreographed and controlled – and we don't want to risk an encounter that might prove to be rather more messy and unpredictable. But perhaps more fundamentally, we undervalue the child within us, and fail to recognise the validity of a childlike approach to Jesus.

Those who come to faith later in life often begin with very little knowledge and understanding of Jesus and how they 'should' relate to him. They feel that they don't know how to read the Bible, or to pray, or to behave in church (be it 'high' or 'low', traditional or contemporary, formal or informal). They look upon those who have been Christians for some years and marvel at their apparent maturity. And so growing in faith becomes a matter of growing in these things – of increasing knowledge and understanding, of daily 'quiet times' and Bible reading and prayer, of regular attendance at Sunday services and other meetings, of involvement in the various 'ministries' of the church.

These are, of course, all good things, but they do not necessarily indicate a true maturing and deepening of our faith. Nonetheless, we tend to value a faith characterised by such things more highly than the 'immature' faith we began with. There are times when we bemoan the fact that we seem to have lost our initial enthusiasm and passion; that 'our first love has grown cold'. Yet rarely do we consider the possibility that our very focus on these signs of maturity might have caused our faith to become jaded. Little children might not have the knowledge, understanding and maturity of adults, but more often than not they are more 'alive', with a greater love of life.

Perhaps the very things that we believe will enable us to come closer to Jesus have actually become a hindrance. Perhaps we need to recover the freedom and joy that comes from approaching him not with the trappings of adulthood, but with the simplicity of a child.

Retreat in the city

Clare Black

Stand in the town square in Chester with your back to the Gothic town hall, the new arts centre on your left, the famous shopping Rows on your right, and the cathedral ahead of you – all just metres away – and you may miss the ancient archway nestled between the Co-op bank and Barclays. In fact, the abbey gateway predates most of what surrounds you, serving as the gate between the town and the abbey courtyard since the twelfth century.

Visitors through the gateway today still remark on the tangible sense of otherness when passing between the town square and what is now known as Abbey Square. Though its medieval monastic buildings have been replaced by elegant Georgian townhouses, the square is still part of the cathedral precinct, and nestled in the far corner, on the site of the old abbey bakehouse and brewery, is a particularly special building.

This building was opened in 1925 as a retreat house, in an adventurous move which nonetheless reflected the growing popularity of retreat nationally. Driven by the cathedral, but with a collaborative effort, the house – which later expanded into the house next door – was converted from a clergy residence, which in its time had housed Charles Kingsley, to a residential retreat house. For years, the retreat house in Chester was well-loved and well-used, until its closure early in this century. Today, large residential retreat centres find themselves challenged by increasing costs and regulation, coupled with declining numbers of those in religious life who were the mainstay of staffing such places. Times have changed.

At Retreat House Chester, we believe that it is a changing context rather than a decline in retreat that presents a challenge. We all know that traditional church attendance is in decline, but research finds that the area of retreats and pilgrimage is enjoying popularity. (Just for fun, see how many times you come across the word 'retreat' this week.) For that tentative personal attraction to retreat, we like the image of Zacchaeus in the tree – removing himself just a little from the crowd and being surprised by what happened next.

As well as being popular, retreat has been shown to be good for us, individually and collectively. It is this recognition that people still want and benefit from retreat that led to the foundation of the charity Retreat House Chester. We offer retreat in the city, in a range of locations including the cathedral, with the aim of reopening the ground floor of the old retreat house for non-residential retreat. With no founding religious order or diocese, we are a non-denominational Christian grassroots charity which survives on the income from its activities and fundraising.

Retreat is as old as the hills, common across cultures and across centuries because it is about something fundamental to human living. We aim to find ways to retreat which work in our own times, offering ways and places to enable as many people as possible to draw on its riches. There is a need for good places to explore spirituality today, and a city-based non-residential retreat house, rooted gently and deeply in Christian spiritual tradition, can be such a place.

City-based is important. In our times, the majority of the UK population lives in towns and cities – and the number is rising. A city-based retreat house plays a part in addressing the needs of modern urban life, helping to make cities the good places they can be. We form our programme around four key areas: find... experience... explore... connect. We offer somewhere for people to *find* a time of stillness and *experience* different ways of developing their reflective nature. They can *explore* spirituality in a broad Christian context, from ancient wisdom to contemporary spirituality. And, importantly, they can *connect* – with one another and with their everyday living.

Non-residential and city-based, Retreat House Chester asserts that spirituality is about every moment of every day: it's about where we are and what we are doing. Zacchaeus came down from the tree and met Christ in his home and in the details of his life. Through retreat in the city, we are able to offer a resource for ready integration of the good things found on retreat with the rest of living. It's a place that helps inner life and outward living meet.

Back in the town square, you'll find yourself in a special place. Although only a small city, Chester has city walls, an estuary river and a canal. It nestles the border with Wales, whose hills shelter us on the horizon. The two main routes between four city gates intersect to form a cross. We have Roman ruins and a strong monastic story, still present in street names. Those streets know wealth and poverty, companionship and isolation. We have industry and business, a university, tourism, a zoo, a racecourse, a cultural calendar and a necessary charitable sector. If you look, you can find spirituality written in Chester's past and present, written into the life of a city.

Email: admin@retreathousechester.co.uk
Website: www.retreathousechester.co.uk
Facebook: www.facebook.com/retreathousechester

BRF Quiet Days

BRF Quiet Days are an ideal way of redressing the balance in our busy lives. Held in peaceful locations around the country, each one is led by an experienced speaker and gives the opportunity to reflect, be silent and pray, and, through it all, to draw closer to God.

Here is the programme for autumn/winter 2018:

Wednesday 26 September: 'Give us this day our daily bread…' led by Debbie Thrower at Old Alresford Place, Alresford, Hampshire SO24 9DH.

Monday 8 October: 'Be still and know… God's love' led by Claire Musters at Holy Trinity Centre, Maldon Road, Wallington S6 8BL.

For further details and to book, please go to **brfonline.org.uk/events-and-quiet-days** or contact us at BRF, 15 The Chambers, Vineyard, Abingdon OX14 3FE; tel: +44 (0)1865 319700.

A book of 24 undated reflections drawing on a range of relevant Bible passages to offer genuine hope and encouragement in anxious times. Encompassing the very human emotions of fear and anxiety, the reflections encourage us to draw comfort and strength from God's word even in those times when he seems silent to us. This book acknowledges that trust and hope in God's goodness doesn't always come easily, but when embraced we gain the strength to face our fear with courage and confidence.

Anxious Times
Carmel Thomason
978 0 85746 660 0 £3.99
brfonline.org.uk

Few would doubt that we live in a wounded and broken world. But God has sent a Saviour, Jesus Christ, who calls us, in the beatitudes, to live an authentic, countercultural lifestyle. By being different we can make a difference, becoming the salt of the earth and the light of the world. Through living the beatitudes, we could make the world a better place.

Living Differently to Make a Difference
The beatitudes and countercultural lifestyle
Will Donaldson
978 0 85746 671 6 £7.99
brfonline.org.uk

Brother Ramon was a much-loved writer and speaker who died in 2000 – a man who delighted in life and people, and who chose solitude to practise the presence of God. This first biography, written by his friend, has warmth and spiritual insight. It tells of his life's pilgrimage, his quest for holiness as a Franciscan friar, his love of God and his influence on others. The selection from his writings which concludes the book illustrates his spiritual journey, his views on ecumenism, contemplative prayer, spirituality, retreats, solitude, quietness and much more.

A Franciscan Way of Life
Brother Ramon's quest for holiness
Arthur Howells
978 0 85746 662 4 £8.99
brfonline.org.uk

To order

Online: **brfonline.org.uk**
Tel.: +44 (0)1865 319700
Mon–Fri 9.15–17.30

Delivery times within the UK are normally 15 working days. Prices are correct at the time of going to press but may change without prior notice.

Title	Price	Qty	Total
Anxious Times	£3.99		
Living Differently to Make a Difference	£7.99		
A Franciscan Way of Life	£8.99		

POSTAGE AND PACKING CHARGES			
Order value	**UK**	**Europe**	**Rest of world**
Under £7.00	£2.00	£5.00	£7.00
£7.00–£29.99	£3.00	£9.00	£15.00
£30.00 and over	FREE	£9.00 + 15% of order value	£15.00 + 20% of order value

Total value of books	
Postage and packing	
Total for this order	

Please complete in BLOCK CAPITALS

Title ________ First name/initials ________________ Surname ________________

Address ____

____ Postcode ________________

Acc. No. ________________________ Telephone ________________________

Email ____

Method of payment

❑ Cheque (made payable to BRF) ❑ MasterCard / Visa

Card no. ☐☐☐☐ ☐☐☐☐ ☐☐☐☐ ☐☐☐☐

Valid from M M Y Y Expires M M Y Y Security code* ☐☐☐

Last 3 digits on the reverse of the card

Signature* ________________________________ Date / ______ / ______ / ______

*ESSENTIAL IN ORDER TO PROCESS YOUR ORDER

Please return this form with the appropriate payment to:

BRF, 15 The Chambers, Vineyard, Abingdon OX14 3FE | enquiries@brf.org.uk

To read our terms and find out about cancelling your order, please visit **brfonline.org.uk/terms**.

QUIET SPACES SUBSCRIPTION FORM

All our Bible reading notes can be ordered online by visiting **biblereadingnotes.org.uk/subscriptions**

If you and a minimum of **four** friends subscribe to ***Quiet Spaces*** or BRF's other Bible reading notes (***New Daylight***, ***Day by Day with God***, ***Guidelines***, ***The Upper Room***), you can form a group. What's so good about being in a group? You pay the price of the notes only – postage is free for delivery to a UK address. (All notes are sent to one address.) All group orders are invoiced. No advance payment is required. For more information, visit **biblereadingnotes.org.uk/group-subscriptions** or contact the BRF office.

Title ___________ First name/initials _____________ Surname ________________________________

Address ____

____ Postcode ____________________

Telephone ________________________ Email ____

INDIVIDUAL SUBSCRIPTION Please send *Quiet Spaces* beginning with the January 2019 / May 2019 / September 2019 issue (*delete as appropriate*):

	Quantity	UK	Europe	Rest of world
(per 3 issues)	☐	☐ £16.95	☐ £25.20	☐ £29.10

Total enclosed £ ________________ (cheques should be made payable to 'BRF')

Please charge my MasterCard / Visa ☐ Debit card ☐ with £ ________________

Card no. ☐☐☐☐ ☐☐☐☐ ☐☐☐☐ ☐☐☐☐

Valid from ☐☐ ☐☐ Expires ☐☐ ☐☐ Security code* ☐☐☐

Last 3 digits on the reverse of the card

Signature* ____ Date ______/______/______

*ESSENTIAL IN ORDER TO PROCESS YOUR ORDER

To set up a Direct Debit, please also complete the Direct Debit instruction on the reverse of this form.

GROUP SUBSCRIPTION (UK only) Please send *Quiet Spaces* beginning with the January 2019 / May 2019 / September 2019 issue (*delete as appropriate*):

Quantity ☐ (Current price per issue: £4.50)

Please invoice me: per issue / annually (*delete as appropriate*).

Please return this form to:

BRF, 15 The Chambers, Vineyard, Abingdon OX14 3FE

To read our terms and find out about cancelling your order, please visit **brfonline.org.uk/terms**.

The Bible Reading Fellowship is a Registered Charity (233280)

QS0318

The Bible Reading Fellowship

Instruction to your bank or building society to pay by Direct Debit

Please fill in the whole form using a ballpoint pen and return it to:
BRF, 15 The Chambers, Vineyard, Abingdon OX14 3FE

Service User Number: | 5 | 5 | 8 | 2 | 2 | 9 |

Name and full postal address of your bank or building society

To: The Manager	Bank/Building Society
Address	
	Postcode

Name(s) of account holder(s)

Branch sort code

Bank/Building Society account number

Reference number

Instruction to your Bank/Building Society
Please pay The Bible Reading Fellowship Direct Debits from the account detailed in this instruction, subject to the safeguards assured by the Direct Debit Guarantee. I understand that this instruction may remain with The Bible Reading Fellowship and, if so, details will be passed electronically to my bank/building society.

Signature(s)

Banks and Building Societies may not accept Direct Debit instructions for some types of account.

DIRECT DEBIT PAYMENT

You can pay for your annual subscription to our Bible reading notes using Direct Debit. You need only give your bank details once, and the payment is made automatically every year until you cancel it. If you would like to pay by Direct Debit, please use the form opposite, entering your BRF account number under 'Reference number'.

You are fully covered by the Direct Debit Guarantee:

The Direct Debit Guarantee

- This Guarantee is offered by all banks and building societies that accept instructions to pay Direct Debits.
- If there are any changes to the amount, date or frequency of your Direct Debit, The Bible Reading Fellowship will notify you 10 working days in advance of your account being debited or as otherwise agreed. If you request The Bible Reading Fellowship to collect a payment, confirmation of the amount and date will be given to you at the time of the request.
- If an error is made in the payment of your Direct Debit, by The Bible Reading Fellowship or your bank or building society, you are entitled to a full and immediate refund of the amount paid from your bank or building society.
- If you receive a refund you are not entitled to, you must pay it back when The Bible Reading Fellowship asks you to.
- You can cancel a Direct Debit at any time by simply contacting your bank or building society. Written confirmation may be required. Please also notify us.

How to encourage Bible reading in your church

BRF has been helping individuals connect with the Bible for over 90 years. We want to support churches as they seek to encourage church members into regular Bible reading.

Order a Bible reading resources pack

This pack is designed to give your church the tools to publicise our Bible reading notes. It includes:

- Sample Bible reading notes for your congregation to try.
- Publicity resources, including a poster.
- A church magazine feature about Bible reading notes.

The pack is free, but we welcome a £5 donation to cover the cost of postage. If you require a pack to be sent outside the UK or require a specific number of sample Bible reading notes, please contact us for postage costs. More information about what the current pack contains is available on our website.

How to order and find out more

- Visit **biblereadingnotes.org.uk/for-churches**.
- Telephone BRF on +44 (0)1865 319700 Mon–Fri 9.15–17.30.
- Write to us at BRF, 15 The Chambers, Vineyard, Abingdon OX14 3FE.

Keep informed about our latest initiatives

We are continuing to develop resources to help churches encourage people into regular Bible reading, wherever they are on their journey. Join our email list at **biblereadingnotes.org.uk/helping-churches** to stay informed about the latest initiatives that your church could benefit from.

Introduce a friend to our notes

We can send information about our notes and current prices for you to pass on. Please contact us.